Oakland Athletics 2021

A Baseball Companion

Edited by Steven Goldman and Bret Sayre

Baseball Prospectus

Craig Brown, Associate Editor
Robert Au, Harry Pavlidis and Amy Pircher, Statistics Editors

Copyright © 2021 by DIY Baseball, LLC.
All rights reserved

This book or any part thereof may not be reproduced or transmitted in any form or by any means, electronic or mechanical, including photocopying, recording, or by any information storage and retrieval system, without permission in writing from the publisher.

Limit of Liability/Disclaimer of Warranty: While the publisher and the author have used their best efforts in preparing this book, they make no representations or warranties with respect to the accuracy or completeness of the contents of this book and specifically disclaim any implied warranties of merchantability or fitness for a particular purpose. No warranty may be created or extended by sales representatives or written sales materials. The advice and strategies contained herein may not be suitable for your situation. You should consult with a professional where appropriate. Neither the publisher nor the author shall be liable for any loss of profit or any other commercial damages, including but not limited to special, incidental, consequential, or other damages.

Library of Congress Cataloging-in-Publication Data:
paperback
ISBN-13: 978-1-950716-63-0

Project Credits
Cover Design: Ginny Searle
Interior Design and Production: Amy Pircher, Robert Au
Layout: Amy Pircher, Robert Au

Baseball icon courtesy of Uberux, from https://www.shareicon.net/author/uberux

Ballpark diagram courtesy of Lou Spirito/THIRTY81 Project, https://thirty81project.com/

Manufactured in the United States of America
10 9 8 7 6 5 4 3 2 1

Table of Contents

Statistical Introduction v

Part 1: Team Analysis

Performance Graphs 3
2020 Team Performance 4
2021 Team Projections 5
Team Personnel 6
Oakland–Alameda County Coliseum Stats 7
Athletics Team Analysis 9

Part 2: Player Analysis

Athletics Player Analysis 14
Athletics Prospects 77

Part 3: Featured Articles

Athletics All-Time Top 10 Players 89
    by Rob Mains

A Taxonomy of 2020 Abnormalities 95
    by Rob Mains

Tranches of WAR 101
    by Russell A. Carleton

Secondhand Sport 107
    by Patrick Dubuque

Steve Dalkowski Dreaming 111
    by Steven Goldman

A Reward For A Functioning Society 115
    by Cory Frontin and Craig Goldstein

Index of Names 119

Statistical Introduction

Sports are, fundamentally, a blend of athletic endeavor and storytelling. Baseball, like any other sport, tells its stories in so many ways: in the arc of a game from the stands or a season from the box scores, in photos, or even in numbers. At Baseball Prospectus, we understand that statistics don't replace observation or any of baseball's stories, but complement everything else that makes the game so much fun.

What stats help us with is with patterns and precision, variance and value. This book can help you learn things you may not see from watching a game or hundred, whether it's the path of a career over time or the breadth of the entire MLB. We'd also never ask you to choose between our numbers and the experience of viewing a game from the cheap seats or the comfort of your home; our publication combines running the numbers with observations and wisdom from some of the brightest minds we can find. But if you *do* want to learn more about the numbers beyond what's on the backs of player jerseys, let us help explain.

Offense

We've revised our methodology for determining batting value. Long-time readers of the book will notice that we've retired True Average in favor of a new metric: Deserved Runs Created Plus (DRC+). Developed by Jonathan Judge and our stats team, this statistic measures everything a player does at the plate–reaching base, hitting for power, making outs, and moving runners over–and puts it on a scale where 100 equals league-average performance. A DRC+ of 150 is terrific, a DRC+ of 100 is average and a DRC+ of 75 means you better be an excellent defender.

DRC+ also does a better job than any of our previous metrics in taking contextual factors into account. The model adjusts for how the park affects performance, but also for things like the talent of the opposing pitcher, value of different types of batted-ball events, league, temperature and other factors. It's able to describe a player's expected offensive contribution than any other statistic we've found over the years, and also does a better job of predicting future performance as well.

The other aspect of run-scoring is baserunning, which we quantify using Baserunning Runs. BRR not only records the value of stolen bases (or getting caught in the act), but also accounts for all the stuff that doesn't show up on the back of a baseball card: a runner's ability to go first to third on a single, or advance on a fly ball.

Defense

Where offensive value is *relatively* easy to identify and understand, defensive value is … not. Over the past dozen years, the sabermetric community has focused mostly on stats based on zone data: a real-live human person records the type of batted ball and estimated landing location, and models are created that give expected outs. From there, you can compare fielders' actual outs to those expected ones. Simple, right?

Unfortunately, zone data has two major issues. First, zone data is recorded by commercial data providers who keep the raw data private unless you pay for it. (All the statistics we build in this book and on our website use public data as inputs.) That hurts our ability to test assumptions or duplicate results. Second, over the years it has become apparent that there's quite a bit of "noise" in zone-based fielding analysis. Sometimes the conclusions drawn from zone data don't hold up to scrutiny, and sometimes the different data provided by different providers don't look anything alike, giving wildly different results. Sometimes the hard-working professional stringers or scorers might unknowingly inflict unconscious bias into the mix: for example good fielders will often be credited with more expected outs despite the data, and ballparks with high press boxes tend to score more line drives than ones with a lower press box.

Enter our Fielding Runs Above Average (FRAA). For most positions, FRAA is built from play-by-play data, which allows us to avoid the subjectivity found in many other fielding metrics. The idea is this: count how many fielding plays are made by a given player and compare that to expected plays for an average fielder at their position (based on pitcher ground ball tendencies and batter handedness). Then we adjust for park and base-out situations.

When it comes to catchers, our methodology is a little different thanks to the laundry list of responsibilities they're tasked with beyond just, well, catching and throwing the ball. By now you've probably heard about "framing" or the art of making umpires more likely to call balls outside the strike zone for strikes. To put this into one tidy number, we incorporate pitch tracking data (for the years it exists) and adjust for important factors like pitcher, umpire, batter and home-field advantage using a mixed-model approach. This grants us a number for how many strikes the catcher is personally adding to (or subtracting from) his pitchers' performance … which we then convert to runs added or lost using linear weights.

Framing is one of the biggest parts of determining catcher value, but we also take into account blocking balls from going past, whether a scorer deems it a passed ball or a wild pitch. We use a similar approach—one that really benefits from the pitch tracking data that tells us what ends up in the dirt and what doesn't. We also include a catcher's ability to prevent stolen bases and how well they field balls in play, and *finally* we come up with our FRAA for catchers.

Pitching

Both pitching and fielding make up the half of baseball that isn't run scoring: run prevention. Separating pitching from fielding is a tough task, and most recent pitching analysis has branched off from Voros McCracken's famous (and controversial) statement, "There is little if any difference among major-league pitchers in their ability to prevent hits on balls hit in the field of play." The research of the analytic community has validated this to some extent, and there are a host of "defense-independent" pitching measures that have been developed to try and extract the effect of the defense behind a hurler from the pitcher's work.

Our solution to this quandary is Deserved Run Average (DRA), our core pitching metric. DRA seeks to evaluate a pitcher's performance, much like earned run average (ERA), the tried-and-true pitching stat you've seen on every baseball broadcast or box score from the past century, but it's very different. To start, DRA takes an event-by-event look at what the pitchers does, and adjusts the value of that event based on different environmental factors like park, batter, catcher, umpire, base-out situation, run differential, inning, defense, home field advantage, pitcher role and temperature. That mixed model gives us a pitcher's expected contribution, similar to what we do for our DRC+ model for hitters and FRAA model for catchers. (Oh, and we also consider the pitcher's effect on basestealing and on balls getting past the catcher.)

DRA is set to the scale of runs allowed per nine innings (RA9) instead of ERA, which makes DRA's scale slightly higher than ERA's. Because of this, for ease of use, we're supplying DRA-, which is much easier for the reader to parse. As with DRC+, DRA- is an "index" stat, meaning instead of using some arbitrary and shifting number to denote what's "good," average is always 100. The reason that it uses a minus rather than a plus is because like ERA, a lower number is better. Therefore a 75 DRA- describes a performance 25 percent better than average, whereas a 150 DRA- means that either a pitcher is getting extremely lucky with their results, or getting ready to try a new pitch.

Since the last time you picked up an edition of this book, we've also made a few minor changes to DRA to make it better. Recent research into "tunneling"—the act of throwing consecutive pitches that appear similar from a batter's point of view until after the swing decision point–data has given us a new contextual factor to account for in DRA: plate distance. This refers to the distance between successive pitches as they approach the plate, and while it has a smaller effect than factors like velocity or whiff rate, it still can help explain pitcher strikeout rate in our model.

Recently Added Descriptive Statistics

Returning to our 2021 edition of the book are a few figures which recently appeared. These numbers may be a little bit more familiar to those of you who have spent some time investigating baseball statistics.

Fastball Percentage

Our fastball percentage (FA%) statistic measures how frequently a pitcher throws a pitch classified as a "fastball," measured as a percentage of overall pitches thrown. We qualify three types of fastballs:

1. The traditional four-seam fastball;
2. The two-seam fastball or sinker;
3. "Hard cutters," which are pitches that have the movement profile of a cut fastball and are used as the pitcher's primary offering or in place of a more traditional fastball.

For example, a pitcher with a FA% of 67 throws any combination of these three pitches about two-thirds of the time.

Whiff Rate

Everybody loves a swing and a miss, and whiff rate (Whiff%) measures how frequently pitchers induce a swinging strike. To calculate Whiff%, we add up all the pitches thrown that ended with a swinging strike, then divide that number by a pitcher's total pitches thrown. Most often, high whiff rates correlate with high strikeout rates (and overall effective pitcher performance).

Called Strike Probability

Called Strike Probability (CSP) is a number that represents the likelihood that all of a pitcher's pitches will be called a strike while controlling for location, pitcher and batter handedness, umpire and count. Here's how it works: on each pitch, our model determines how many times (out of 100) that a similar pitch was called for a strike given those factors mentioned above, and when normalized for each batter's strike zone. Then we average the CSP for all pitches thrown by a pitcher in a season, and that gives us the yearly CSP percentage you see in the stats boxes.

As you might imagine, pitchers with a higher CSP are more likely to work in the zone, where pitchers with a lower CSP are likely locating their pitches outside the normal strike zone, for better or for worse.

Projections

Many of you aren't turning to this book just for a look at what a player has done, but for a look at what a player is going to do: the PECOTA projections. PECOTA, initially developed by Nate Silver (who has moved on to greater fame as a political analyst), consists of three parts:

1. Major-league equivalencies, which use minor-league statistics to project how a player will perform in the major leagues;
2. Baseline forecasts, which use weighted averages and regression to the mean to estimate a player's current true talent level; and
3. Aging curves, which uses the career paths of comparable players to estimate how a player's statistics are likely to change over time.

With all those important things covered, let's take a look at what's in the book this year.

Team Prospectus

Most of this book is composed of team chapters, with one for each of the 30 major-league franchises. On the first page of each chapter, you'll see a box that contains some of the key statistics for each team as well as a very inviting stadium diagram.

We start with the team name, their unadjusted 2020 win-loss record, and their divisional ranking. Beneath that are a host of other team statistics. **Pythag** presents an adjusted 2020 winning percentage, calculated by taking runs scored per game (**RS/G**) and runs allowed per game (**RA/G**) for the team, and running them through a version of Bill James' Pythagorean formula that was refined and improved by David Smyth and Brandon Heipp. (The formula is called "Pythagenpat," which is equally fun to type and to say.)

Next up is **DRC+**, described earlier, to indicate the overall hitting ability of the team either above or below league-average. Run prevention on the pitching side is covered by **DRA** (also mentioned earlier) and another metric: Fielding Independent Pitching (**FIP**), which calculates another ERA-like statistic based on strikeouts, walks, and home runs recorded. Defensive Efficiency Rating (**DER**) tells us the percentage of balls in play turned into outs for the team, and is a quick fielding shorthand that rounds out run prevention.

After that, we have several measures related to roster composition, as opposed to on-field performance. **B-Age** and **P-Age** tell us the average age of a team's batters and pitchers, respectively. **Payroll** is the combined team payroll for all on-field players, and Doug Pappas' Marginal Dollars per Marginal Win (**M$/MW**) tells us how much money a team spent to earn production above replacement level.

Oakland Athletics 2021

Next to each of these stats, we've listed each team's MLB rank in that category from first to 30th. In this, first always indicates a positive outcome and 30th a negative outcome, except in the case of salary—first is highest.

After the franchise statistics, we share a few items about the team's home ballpark. There's the aforementioned diagram of the park's dimensions (including distances to the outfield wall), a graphic showing the height of the wall from the left-field pole to the right-field pole, and a table showing three-year park factors for the stadium. The park factors are displayed as indexes where 100 is average, 110 means that the park inflates the statistic in question by 10 percent, and 90 means that the park deflates the statistic in question by 10 percent.

On the second page of each team chapter, you'll find three graphs. The first is **Payroll History** and helps you see how the team's payroll has compared to the MLB and divisional average payrolls over time. Payroll figures are current as of January 1, 2021; with so many free agents still unsigned as of this writing, the final 2021 figure will likely be significantly different for many teams. (In the meantime, you can always find the most current data at Baseball Prospectus' Cot's Baseball Contracts page.)

The second graph is **Future Commitments** and helps you see the team's future outlays, if any.

The third graph is **Farm System Ranking** and displays how the Baseball Prospectus prospect team has ranked the organization's farm system since 2007.

After the graphs, we have a **Personnel** section that lists many of the important decision-makers and upper-level field and operations staff members for the franchise, as well as any former Baseball Prospectus staff members who are currently part of the organization. (In very rare circumstances, someone might be on both lists!)

Position Players

After all that information and a thoughtful bylined essay covering each team, we present our player comments. These are also bylined, but due to frequent franchise shifts during the offseason, our bylines are more a rough guide than a perfect accounting of who wrote what.

Each player is listed with the major-league team that employed him as of early January 2021. If a player changed teams after that point via free agency, trade, or any other method, you'll be able to find them in the chapter for their previous squad.

As an example, take a look at the player comment for Padres shortstop Fernando Tatis Jr.: the stat block that accompanies his written comment is at the top of this page. First we cover biographical information (age is as of June 30, 2021) before moving onto the stats themselves. Our statistic columns include standard identifying information like **YEAR**, **TEAM**, **LVL** (level of affiliated play) and **AGE** before getting into the numbers. Next, we provide raw, untranslated

Fernando Tatis Jr. SS

Born: 01/02/99 Age: 22 Bats: R Throws: R
Height: 6'3" Weight: 217 Origin: International Free Agent, 2015

YEAR	TEAM	LVL	AGE	PA	R	2B	3B	HR	RBI	BB	K	SB	CS	AVG/OBP/SLG
2018	SA	AA	19	394	77	22	4	16	43	33	109	16	5	.286/.355/.507
2019	SD	MLB	20	372	61	13	6	22	53	30	110	16	6	.317/.379/.590
2020	SD	MLB	21	257	50	11	2	17	45	27	61	11	3	.277/.366/.571
2021 FS	SD	MLB	22	600	95	24	4	31	81	50	165	17	8	.263/.331/.499
2021 DC	SD	MLB	22	628	100	25	4	32	85	53	173	19	8	.263/.331/.499

Comparables: Darryl Strawberry, Bo Bichette, Ronald Acuña Jr.

YEAR	TEAM	LVL	AGE	PA	DRC+	BABIP	BRR	FRAA	WARP
2018	SA	AA	19	394	136	.370	3.0	SS(83): -1.9	2.4
2019	SD	MLB	20	372	118	.410	7.1	SS(83): 0.9	3.4
2020	SD	MLB	21	257	126	.306	0.7	SS(57): -5.5	0.9
2021 FS	SD	MLB	22	600	126	.318	1.7	SS -1	3.9
2021 DC	SD	MLB	22	628	126	.318	1.8	SS -1	4.0

numbers like you might find on the back of your dad's baseball cards: **PA** (plate appearances), **R** (runs), **2B** (doubles), **3B** (triples), **HR** (home runs), **RBI** (runs batted in), **BB** (walks), **K** (strikeouts), **SB** (stolen bases) and **CS** (caught stealing).

Following the basic stats is **Whiff%** (whiff rate), which denotes how often, when a batter swings, he fails to make contact with the ball. Another way to think of this number is an inverse of a hitter's contact rate.

Next, we have unadjusted "slash" statistics: **AVG** (batting average), **OBP** (on-base percentage) and **SLG** (slugging percentage). Following the slash line is **DRC+** (Deserved Runs Created Plus), which we described earlier as total offensive expected contribution compared to the league average.

BABIP (batting average on balls in play) tells us how often a ball in play fell for a hit, and can help us identify whether a batter may have been lucky or not ... but note that high BABIPs also tend to follow the great hitters of our time, as well as speedy singles hitters who put the ball on the ground.

The next item is **BRR** (Baserunning Runs), which covers all of a player's baserunning accomplishments including (but not limited to) swiped bags and failed attempts. Next is **FRAA** (Fielding Runs Above Average), which also includes the number of games previously played at each position noted in parentheses. Multi-position players have only their two most frequent positions listed here, but their total FRAA number reflects all positions played.

Our last column here is **WARP** (Wins Above Replacement Player). WARP estimates the total value of a player, which means for hitters it takes into account hitting runs above average (calculated using the DRC+ model), BRR and FRAA. Then, it makes an adjustment for positions played and gives the player a credit

Oakland Athletics 2021

for plate appearances based upon the difference between "replacement level"—which is derived from the quality of players added to a team's roster after the start of the season–and the league average.

The final line just below the stats box is **PECOTA** data, which is discussed further in a following section.

Catchers

Catchers are a special breed, and thus they have earned their own separate box which displays some of the defensive metrics that we've built just for them. As an example, let's check out Yasmani Grandal.

YEAR	TEAM	P. COUNT	FRM RUNS	BLK RUNS	THRW RUNS	TOT RUNS
2018	LAD	16816	15.7	0.8	0.1	16.5
2019	MIL	18740	19.4	1.8	-0.1	21.1
2020	CHW	4830	3.7	0.3	-0.2	3.8
2021	CHW	14430	16.7	-0.6	1.0	17.1
2021	CHW	14430	16.7	0.4	1.0	18.0

The **YEAR** and **TEAM** columns match what you'd find in the other stat box. **P. COUNT** indicates the number of pitches thrown while the catcher was behind the plate, including swinging strikes, fouls and balls in play. **FRM RUNS** is the total run value the catcher provided (or cost) his team by influencing the umpire to call strikes where other catchers did not. **BLK RUNS** expresses the total run value above or below average for the catcher's ability to prevent wild pitches and passed balls. **THRW RUNS** is calculated using a similar model as the previous two statistics, and it measures a catcher's ability to throw out basestealers but also to dissuade them from testing his arm in the first place. It takes into account factors like the pitcher (including his delivery and pickoff move) and baserunner (who could be as fast as Billy Hamilton or as slow as Yonder Alonso). **TOT RUNS** is the sum of all of the previous three statistics.

Pitchers

Let's give our pitchers a turn, using 2020 AL Cy Young winner Shane Bieber as our example. Take a look at his stat block: the first line and the **YEAR**, **TEAM**, **LVL** and **AGE** columns are the same as in the position player example earlier.

Here too, we have a series of columns that display raw, unadjusted statistics compiled by the pitcher over the course of a season: **W** (wins), **L** (losses), **SV** (saves), **G** (games pitched), **GS** (games started), **IP** (innings pitched), **H** (hits allowed) and **HR** (home runs allowed). Next we have two statistics that are rates: **BB/9** (walks per nine innings) and **K/9** (strikeouts per nine innings), before returning to the unadjusted K (strikeouts).

Next up is **GB%** (ground ball percentage), which is the percentage of all batted balls that were hit on the ground, including both outs and hits. Remember, this is based on observational data and subject to human error, so please approach this with a healthy dose of skepticism.

BABIP (batting average on balls in play) is calculated using the same methodology as it is for position players, but it often tells us more about a pitcher than it does a hitter. With pitchers, a high BABIP is often due to poor defense or bad luck, and can often be an indicator of potential rebound, and a low BABIP may be cause to expect performance regression. (A typical league-average BABIP is close to .290-.300.)

The metrics **WHIP** (walks plus hits per inning pitched) and **ERA** (earned run average) are old standbys: WHIP measures walks and hits allowed on a per-inning basis, while ERA measures earned runs on a nine-inning basis. Neither of these stats are translated or adjusted.

DRA- (Deserved Run Average) was described at length earlier, and measures how the pitcher "deserved" to perform compared to other pitchers. Please note that since we lack all the data points that would make for a "real" DRA for minor-league events, the DRA- displayed for minor league partial-seasons is based off of different data. (That data is a modified version of our cFIP metric, which you can find more information about on our website.)

Shane Bieber   RHP

Born: 05/31/95   Age: 26   Bats: R   Throws: R
Height: 6'3"   Weight: 200   Origin: Round 4, 2016 Draft (#122 overall)

YEAR	TEAM	LVL	AGE	W	L	SV	G	GS	IP	H	HR	BB/9	K/9	K	GB%	BABIP
2018	AKR	AA	23	3	0	0	5	5	31	26	1	0.3	8.7	30	47.3%	.278
2018	COL	AAA	23	3	1	0	8	8	48^2	30	3	1.1	8.7	47	52.0%	.227
2018	CLE	MLB	23	11	5	0	20	19	114^2	130	13	1.8	9.3	118	46.2%	.356
2019	CLE	MLB	24	15	8	0	34	33	214^1	186	31	1.7	10.9	259	44.4%	.298
2020	CLE	MLB	25	8	1	0	12	12	77^1	46	7	2.4	14.2	122	48.4%	.267
2021 FS	CLE	MLB	26	10	6	0	26	26	150	121	18	2.1	11.7	195	45.5%	.297
2021 DC	CLE	MLB	26	14	7	0	30	30	196.7	159	24	2.1	11.7	257	45.5%	.297

Comparables: Luis Severino, Danny Salazar, Joe Musgrove

YEAR	TEAM	LVL	AGE	WHIP	ERA	DRA-	WARP	MPH	FB%	WHF	CSP
2018	AKR	AA	23	0.87	1.16	61	0.9				
2018	COL	AAA	23	0.74	1.66	69	1.2				
2018	CLE	MLB	23	1.33	4.55	74	2.6	94.7	57.4%	26.2%	
2019	CLE	MLB	24	1.05	3.28	75	4.9	94.4	45.8%	30.8%	
2020	CLE	MLB	25	0.87	1.63	53	2.6	95.3	53.6%	40.7%	
2021 FS	CLE	MLB	26	1.04	2.44	64	4.4	94.7	50.0%	33.2%	44.2%
2021 DC	CLE	MLB	26	1.04	2.44	64	5.8	94.7	50.0%	33.2%	44.2%

Just like with hitters, **WARP** (Wins Above Replacement Player) is a total value metric that puts pitchers of all stripes on the same scale as position players. We use DRA as the primary input for our calculation of WARP. You might notice that relief pitchers (due to their limited innings) may have a lower WARP than you were expecting or than you might see in other WARP-like metrics. WARP does not take leverage into account, just the actions a pitcher performs and the expected value of those actions … which ends up judging high-leverage relief pitchers differently than you might imagine given their prestige and market value.

MPH gives you the pitcher's 95th percentile velocity for the noted season, in order to give you an idea of what the *peak* fastball velocity a pitcher possesses. Since this comes from our pitch-tracking data, it is not publicly available for minor-league pitchers.

Finally, we display the three new pitching metrics we described earlier. **FB%** (fastball percentage) gives you the percentage of fastballs thrown out of all pitches. **WHF** (whiff rate) tells you the percentage of swinging strikes induced out of all pitches. **CSP** (called strike probability) expresses the likelihood of all pitches thrown to result in a called strike, after controlling for factors like handedness, umpire, pitch type, count and location.

PECOTA

All players have PECOTA projections for 2021, as well as a set of other numbers that describe the performance of comparable players according to PECOTA. All projections for 2021 are for the player at the date we went to press in early January and are projected into the league and park context as indicated by the team abbreviation. (Note that players at very low levels of the minors are too unpredictable to assess using these numbers.) All PECOTA projected statistics represent a player's projected major-league performance.

How we're doing that is a little different this season. There are really two different values that go into the final stat line that you see for PECOTA: How a player performs, and how much playing time he'll be given to perform it. In the past we've estimated playing time based on each team's roster and depth charts, and we'll continue to do that. These projections are denoted as **2021 DC**.

But in many cases, a player won't be projected for major-league playing time; most of the time this is because they aren't projected to be major-league players at all, but still developing as prospects. Or perhaps a player will provide Triple-A depth, only to have an opportunity open up because of injury. For these purposes, we're also supplying a second projection, labeled **2021 FS**, or full season. This is what we would project the player to provide in 600 plate appearances or 150 innings pitched.

Below the projections are the player's three highest-scoring comparable players as determined by PECOTA. All comparables represent a snapshot of how the listed player was performing at the same age as the current player, so if a

23-year-old pitcher is compared to Bartolo Colón, he's actually being compared to a 23-year-old Colón, not the version that pitched for the Rangers in 2018, nor to Colón's career as a whole.

A few points about pitcher projections. First, we aren't yet projecting peak velocity, so that column will be blank in the PECOTA lines. Second, projecting DRA is trickier than evaluating past performance, because it is unclear how deserving each pitcher will be of his anticipated outcomes. However, we know that another DRA-related statistic–contextual FIP or cFIP-estimates future run scoring very well. So for PECOTA, the projected DRA- figures you see are based on the past cFIPs generated by the pitcher and comparable players over time, along with the other factors described above.

If you're familiar with PECOTA, then you'll have noticed that the projection system often appears bullish on players coming off a bad year and bearish on players coming off a good year. (This is because the system weights several previous seasons, not just the most recent one.) In addition, we publish the 50th percentile projections for each player–which is smack in the middle of the range of projected production—which tends to mean PECOTA stat lines don't often have extreme results like 40 home runs or 250 strikeouts in a given season. In essence, PECOTA doesn't project very many extreme seasons.

Managers

After all those wonderful team chapters, we've got statistics for each big-league manager, all of whom are organized by alphabetical order. Here you'll find a block including an extraordinary amount of information collected from each manager's entire career. For more information on the acronyms and what they mean, please visit the Glossary at www.baseballprospectus.com.

There is one important metric that we'd like to call attention to, and you'll find it next to each manager's name: **wRM+** (weighted reliever management plus). Developed by Rob Arthur and Rian Watt, wRM+ investigates how good a manager is at using their best relievers during the moments of highest leverage, using both our proprietary DRA metric as well as Leverage Index. wRM+ is scaled to a league average of 100, and a wRM+ of 105 indicates that relievers were used approximately five percent "better" than average. On the other hand, a wRM+ of 95 would tell us the team used its relievers five percent "worse" than the average team.

While wRM+ does not have an extremely strong correlation with a manager, it is statistically significant; this means that a manager is not *entirely* responsible for a team's wRM+, but does have some effect on that number.

Part 1: Team Analysis

Performance Graphs

Payroll History (in millions)

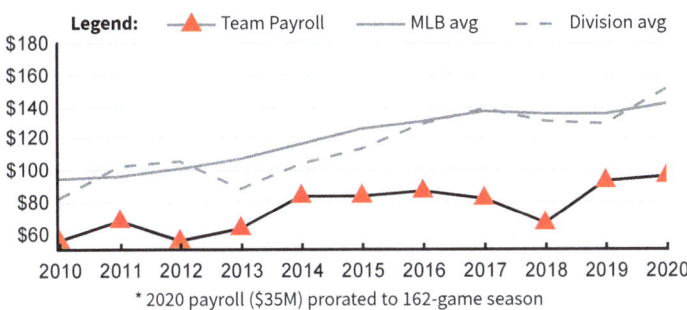

Future Commitments (in millions)

Farm System Ranking

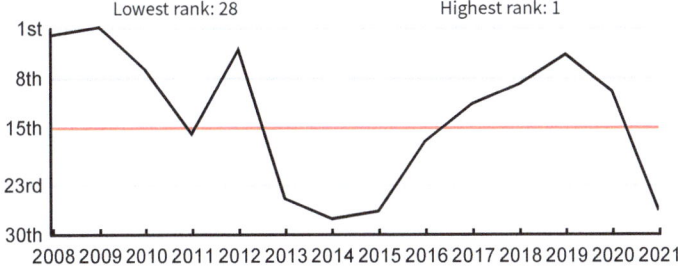

2020 Team Performance

ACTUAL STANDINGS

Team	W	L	Pct
OAK	**36**	**24**	**0.600**
HOU	29	31	0.483
SEA	27	33	0.450
LAA	26	34	0.433
TEX	22	38	0.367

dWIN% STANDINGS

Team	W	L	Pct
OAK	**29**	**31**	**0.499**
LAA	29	31	0.497
HOU	28	32	0.472
SEA	22	38	0.370
TEX	18	42	0.304

TOP HITTERS

Player	WARP
Ramón Laureano	1.7
Mark Canha	1.6
Marcus Semien	1.6

TOP PITCHERS

Player	WARP
Chris Bassitt	1.0
Sean Manaea	0.9
Jesús Luzardo	0.8

VITAL STATISTICS

Statistic Name	Value	Rank
Pythagenpat	.576	7th
dWin%	.499	9th
Runs Scored per Game	4.57	16th
Runs Allowed per Game	3.87	5th
Deserved Runs Created Plus	103	12th
Deserved Run Average Minus	98	15th
Fielding Independent Pitching	4.04	8th
Defensive Efficiency Rating	.705	11th
Batter Age	28.6	12th
Pitcher Age	29.8	22nd
Payroll	$35.0M	26th
Marginal $ per Marginal Win	$1.0M	3rd

2021 Team Projections

PROJECTED STANDINGS

Team	W	L	Pct	+/-
HOU	92.5	69.5	0.571	14
There's reason to be skeptical of the starting pitching depth, but this team will score plenty of runs.				
LAA	86.2	75.8	0.532	16
Still buying pitching from the bargain bin despite a new GM, they lack the depth to be great, but if the stars stay healthy, they'll be good.				
OAK	**82.2**	**79.8**	**0.507**	**-15**
Free-agent departures in the outfield, infield, and bullpen leave them scrambling for coverage despite Matts Chapman and Olson.				
SEA	70.7	91.3	0.436	-2
The rebuild should be nearly over, but will go on for at least another year after a shockingly silent winter.				
TEX	66.8	95.2	0.412	7
A team in total, chaotic transition, but the kids could be fun to watch.				

TOP PROJECTED HITTERS

Player	WARP
Ramón Laureano	3.9
Matt Olson	3.1
Mark Canha	3.1

TOP PROJECTED PITCHERS

Player	WARP
Sean Manaea	2.0
Jesús Luzardo	1.7
Frankie Montas	1.7

FARM SYSTEM REPORT

Top Prospect	Number of Top 101 Prospects
A.J. Puk	0

KEY DEDUCTIONS

Player	WARP
Tommy La Stella	2.3
Marcus Semien	2.3
Mike Minor	1.9
Robbie Grossman	1.5
Liam Hendriks	1.4
Joakim Soria	0.8
Khris Davis	0.6
Jonah Heim	0.3

KEY ADDITIONS

Player	WARP
Elvis Andrus	1.3
Ka'ai Tom	0.6
Adam Kolarek	0.5

Team Personnel

Executive Vice President of Baseball Operations
Billy Beane

General Manager
David Forst

Assistant General Manager, Pro Scouting & Player Personnel
Dan Feinstein

Assistant General Manager/Director of Player Personnel
Billy Owens

Manager
Bob Melvin

Oakland-Alameda County Coliseum Stats

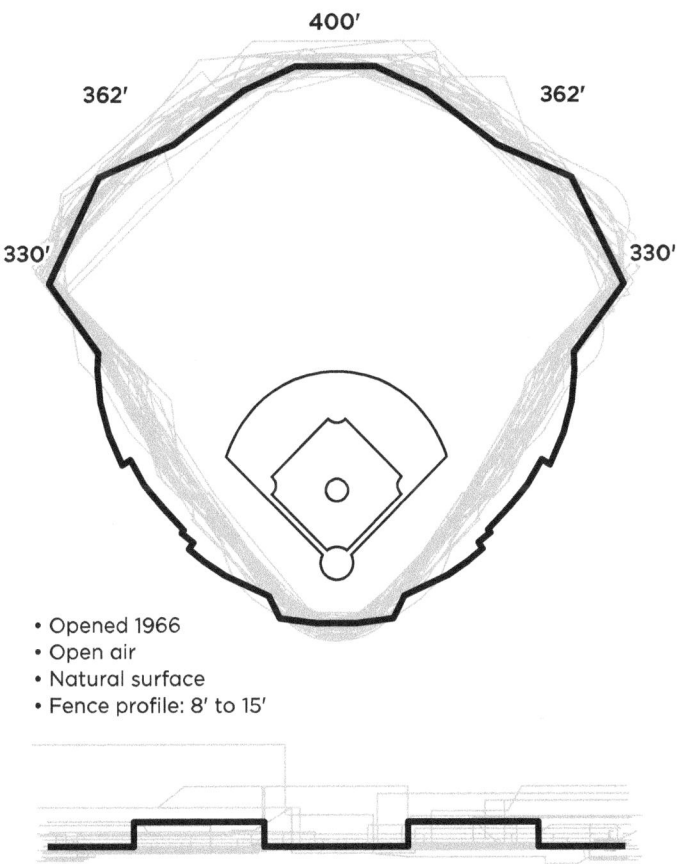

- Opened 1966
- Open air
- Natural surface
- Fence profile: 8' to 15'

Three-Year Park Factors

Runs	Runs/RH	Runs/LH	HR/RH	HR/LH
98	100	94	96	93

Athletics Team Analysis

Stay.

In the baseball world, where each fan base has layers of its own inside jokes printed on T-shirts, from season-long slogans to sly references long forgotten from a 14-inning June affair some number of years back, it's hard to imagine any as personal, as desperate, as meaningful as this one. A green background with gold letters, all stock caps except that distinctive A, differentiated from the blocky, red varieties in Arizona and Orange County, and even the other cursive one from Atlanta, it is unmistakable to any baseball fan.

The word is part demand, part plea. It's not about winning today, or in October. It's not some cute play on words. It's as simple and intrinsic as any aspect of A's fandom—the understanding of and constant, low-grade anxiety driven by the possibility that the team might be snatched away and relocated to some other city with shinier things to offer. That someday, there may not be games to win, or even to show up and enjoy a few beers and brats while losing. It's Joel Barish pleading with Clementine Kruczynski in a darkened hallway at the end of "Eternal Sunshine of the Spotless Mind," knowing there's no storybook ending, that this will always be imperfect, that things may well be destined to fail. OK. Just stay.

Because as bad as things ever looked, as the prospect of a new ballpark was dangled, then snatched away time after time, as star after star found greener pastures elsewhere, at least the A's had Billy Beane.

After never achieving his perceived potential on the field, Beane hung up his spikes in 1990 and took a role in the front office with the Athletics as an advance scout. In the 23 years since Beane ascended to general manager, the A's have made the playoffs 11 times, winning seven AL West titles. They have won 230 games more than they have lost. The only teams with more regular season wins in that span: the Braves, Cardinals, Dodgers, Red Sox and Yankees.

In all, Beane spent has more than 30 years with the A's, building a consistent winner, driving the game's statistical and player analysis revolution, and inspiring a best-selling and oft-misunderstood book and film still referenced and riffed off of in broadcasts today, nearly two decades after it was written.

Thirty years. Thirty years is far more than a generation in baseball. It's a lifetime. Thirty years ago, fresh off three straight runs to the Fall Classic, the now-notoriously-frugal Oakland Athletics had the highest payroll in baseball.

Thirty years before that, they were in Kansas City. Thirty years before that, in Philadelphia. Thirty years before that, they were playing their inaugural season as a charter member of the American League.

For an executive with so much upheaval built into the ethos of his roster management, Beane's own stability has been no small achievement. He knew his shit didn't work in the playoffs, yet still he soldiered on. He came back, year after year, to try again. As other teams cycled through GMs and rebuilds, he found a way to compete, more often than not.

His was a philosophy built around patience. Sure, in a practical sense it was about working long counts, drawing walks, forcing a pitcher to beat you multiple times in the same at-bat, grinding agonizing at-bats and stacking high pitch counts at all times, pushing opposing hurlers out of their comfort zones and toward fatigue and error. It was about wringing out the guy the opponent wanted on the mound to get to the guys they least wanted out there, as early as possible; knives out for the fifth or sixth inning, ready to filet the soft underbelly of the bullpen; to build a lead into the late frames, as the heavy, wet marine layer crept into the East Bay night to suck the life out of any would-be late game heroics from the visitors.

So, too, was patience the philosophy of A's fandom. Patience was their virtue, within seasons and without. Patience through slow starts would be rewarded with scalding summer streaks, including the Miguel Tejada-fueled fever dream of 2002, punctuated by Scott Hatteberg's indelible blast. Patience waiting for prospects to mature and matriculate to the big leagues. Patience for the next window to open. Patience, watching the stars of that window walk away in free agency, watching the front office trade the others to get enough of a return of minor league talent to flip the hourglass over again, to watch and wait once more.

Oakland has waited for another title since the year Beane left the playing field for the front office. Amid all that chaos, the constant turnover and heartbreak, the Godot of a new ballpark, he was the constant. In Billy we trusted.

The original screenplay for "Moneyball" involved an animated Bill James explaining sabermetric principles to the audience and we can thank the baseball gods that never came to fruition. But the chronological frame of story—from the 2001 postseason through the 2002 postseason—failed to provide the redemptive arc from failure to success that we usually demand of our sports movies. The A's lost in the division series, in five games, both times (as well as both the year prior, and the year after this span; truly Sisyphusian). So the Hollywood framing settled on Beane's decision, both for baseball and his family, to turn down the money, and the Red Sox, and to stay.

But A's fans are now facing the prospect of the alternate ending, Beane himself leaving, and for Boston no less. In October, it was reported that Beane's new venture capital group, Redball Acquisition Corp., was pursuing a 20-25 percent stake in Fenway Sports Group. Yes, Fenway, as in the Red Sox and other professional sports holdings, owned by the same John Henry who nearly lured Beane away 18 years prior. If the deal goes through, with Beane attached, it will mean the end of his time in Oakland, as he'll be forced to sell his ownership stake with the A's.

Of course, the Beane era was always going to come to an end eventually. But the fact that he stayed despite Henry's offer in 2002 to make him the highest-paid GM in baseball, despite the multiple rebuilds and reloads in the years since, despite the trauma of four straight Game 5 eliminations and the singular horror of the 2014 AL Wild Card Game, it felt like he might just stay forever. Or until the A's won a title. Or, at least, until they secured a new stadium.

Never mind that Beane's been in more of an executive role the last few years. His presence has defined the club's existence for as long as anyone in the game. But if Beane's done with all this, if he's given up without ever achieving a title, or even a formal plan for that elusive ballpark, what are A's fans left with?

Whatever the A's have been—have meant—to baseball, begins with Beane. Their methods have been copied and improved upon and combined with more money to more success all over the league. First Theo and the Red Sox, then countless other copycats, leading to Moneyball's final form, the McKinsey-steeped Astros. They reflect back every bit of optimization the A's initially brought to the sport, but in grander and more grotesque ways, like the soulless, alien mimics produced in The Shimmer of "Annihilation."

Nietzche told us to beware of fighting with monsters, lest we become monsters ourselves. Maybe the fun of trying to outsmart and outmaneuver everyone else, to succeed in spite of the limitations placed upon him, has been extinguished for Beane. Maybe it has for all of us.

After all, even Theo—who spent less than a decade each in his championship runs with both the Red Sox and the Cubs—has unexpectedly left his post and the sport as a whole, to walk the earth or hide out in the Jundland Wastes of Tatooine. Beane alone stepping away is momentous enough; add Theo's self-exile to the mix, and you're looking at a seismic shift among the power players who have shifted the way we think about the sport.

Michael Lewis' "Moneyball" hit the shelves in bookstores on June 17, 2003, 25 days after an unknown Tennessean everyman with a beer belly, a goatee and a name that would be laughed out of any Hollywood pitch meeting upended the poker world. Chris Moneymaker's stunning success, turning a $40 online qualifier entry into the grandest prize in the game, changed Texas Hold 'Em and poker in America forever. Where once there was easy money for the seasoned pros to pick off, suddenly a wave of sharp young minds, the same kinds of Ivy League quants that would begin to populate front offices around MLB, were plying their skills to swipe the shirts and annual vacation budgets from unsuspecting Vegas tourists and novices online all over the world.

Oakland Athletics 2021

The same human evaluation that scouting departments rely upon was present in poker as well, the eye-test still able to find tells a computer would never see. But it quickly became apparent that the math was more important, and those able to sort the data and apply its lessons most efficiently would win in the long run. Poker, like the baseball season, is a marathon. And the same way that the market inefficiency targeting principles of "Moneyball" soon commanded front office decision-making around the league, so did Game Theory Optimal among poker players. Now, even if you're armed with the best knowledge and tactics, so is nearly everyone else.

One thing has differentiated Beane's approach from that of his acolytes: Even as the Marlins popularized the complete, years-long teardowns that dictate team behavior, and Cleveland proved themselves trendsetters by backing off spending to get just worse enough to remain competitive, Beane has tried to find ways to win every year where it was possible, never enduring more than three straight losing campaigns, cycling through the ideas of rebuilds within seasons and offseasons. The A's have made efforts to compete, to try their best, if they have had any chance of making the postseason, but they've also happily sold the farm without a second thought once those chances were reasonably gone to accelerate their next competitive window. They've done things as cheaply as they could, but there has been no reason to believe they haven't tried to squeeze as many wins as possible out of the rosters they've assembled.

Maybe Beane's approach was always soulless arbitrage, but at least it seemed to be in the service of putting the best possible team on the field within the constraints placed upon him. Whether or not ownership was being honest about the limits of those constraints, the baseball operations themselves always felt transparent. It always felt like they were trying, that they were always upholding the social contract between a major league baseball team and its fans. There was never any shame in wearing green and gold, a not insignificant qualifier in today's game.

In many ways, it's easy for A's fans to be hopeful about the future, because that's all they've ever had. There are transcendent young stars at the corner infield spots and fireballing southpaws on the brink of maturing into front-line starters. But it's simultaneously impossible not to be nervous about that same future—as uncertain as ever, with slashes to payroll both on the field and in the front office, with stadium plans still in limbo, with the sport still accounting for the losses from the pandemic—whether Beane chooses to leave or decides, once more, to stay.

—*Noah Frank is a writer and editor in Washington, D.C.*

Part 2: Player Analysis

Oakland Athletics 2021

PLAYER COMMENTS WITH GRAPHS

Elvis Andrus   SS
Born: 08/26/88   Age: 32   Bats: R   Throws: R
Height: 6'0"   Weight: 210   Origin: International Free Agent, 2005

YEAR	TEAM	LVL	AGE	PA	R	2B	3B	HR	RBI	BB	K	SB	CS	AVG/OBP/SLG
2018	TEX	MLB	29	428	53	20	3	6	33	28	66	5	3	.256/.308/.367
2019	TEX	MLB	30	648	81	27	4	12	72	34	96	31	8	.275/.313/.393
2020	TEX	MLB	31	111	11	5	0	3	7	8	15	3	1	.194/.252/.330
2021 FS	OAK	MLB	32	600	70	27	2	12	59	41	98	20	7	.256/.311/.384
2021 DC	OAK	MLB	32	554	65	25	2	11	55	38	90	18	7	.256/.311/.384

Comparables: Jason Bartlett, Tom Foley, Kurt Stillwell

    If you google Andrus, the People Also Ask section provides "What happened to Elvis Andrus?" as the number one response. It's a fair question. Were they querying the fate of a late-career power surge that helped him maintain his grip on shortstop, despite eroding efensive skills? Perhaps the question was referring to the balky back that kept Andrus sidelined for most of the season. Or maybe it was an attempt to find another clip of dugout shenanigans featuring former teammate Adrian Beltre. There was a time when a Texas youth movement centered on him, but now he's the aging veteran with two years and $28.5 million unpaid, and a team at least that many years away from contention. Manager Chris Woodward already assigned the starting shortstop job to Isiah Kiner-Falefa, signaling the end of an era in which Andrus has served as a fixture for the last dozen Opening Days. Maybe a more appropriate question is, "What happened to the last 12 years?"

YEAR	TEAM	LVL	AGE	PA	DRC+	BABIP	BRR	FRAA	WARP
2018	TEX	MLB	29	428	90	.292	0.5	SS(97): -6.4	0.8
2019	TEX	MLB	30	648	88	.305	2.0	SS(146): 1.0	2.4
2020	TEX	MLB	31	111	86	.200	-0.1	SS(29): -0.2	0.1
2021 FS	OAK	MLB	32	600	94	.289	1.3	SS -1	1.4
2021 DC	OAK	MLB	32	554	94	.289	1.2	SS -1	1.3

Elvis Andrus, continued

Batted Ball Distribution

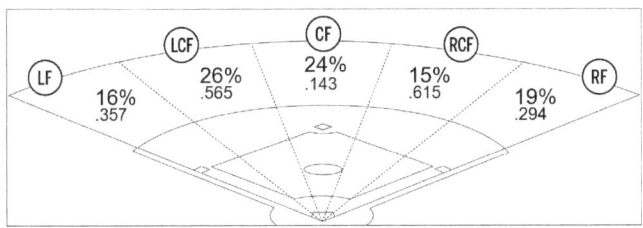

Strike Zone vs LHP   Strike Zone vs RHP

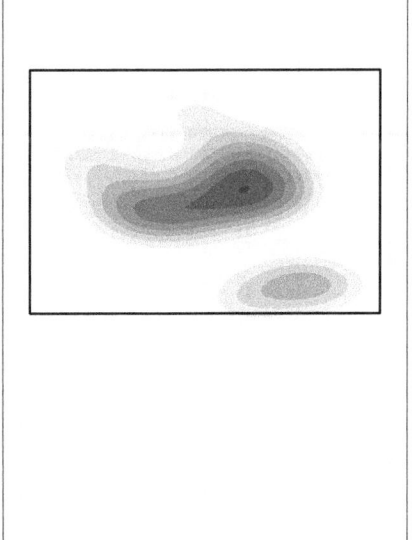

Athletics Player Analysis - 15

Oakland Athletics 2021

Mark Canha OF
Born: 02/15/89 Age: 32 Bats: R Throws: R
Height: 6'2" Weight: 209 Origin: Round 7, 2010 Draft (#227 overall)

YEAR	TEAM	LVL	AGE	PA	R	2B	3B	HR	RBI	BB	K	SB	CS	AVG/OBP/SLG
2018	OAK	MLB	29	411	60	22	0	17	52	34	87	1	2	.249/.328/.449
2019	OAK	MLB	30	497	80	16	3	26	58	67	107	3	2	.273/.396/.517
2020	OAK	MLB	31	243	32	12	2	5	33	37	54	4	0	.246/.387/.408
2021 FS	OAK	MLB	32	600	79	25	1	23	75	65	149	3	2	.237/.343/.434
2021 DC	OAK	MLB	32	584	77	25	1	22	73	63	145	3	2	.237/.343/.434

Comparables: Alex Gordon, Jason Kubel, Greg Vaughn

One unsung casualty of the pandemic upending reality was that of content for Canha's Instagram account, @bigleaguefoodie. Before the pandemic ended in-restaurant dining, Canha uploaded meal pics from stops all over the country to his 20,000-plus followers. Apart from some frankly cruel pictures of ballpark food, the feed largely went dark throughout 2020. Canha's bat, though, didn't, despite what might be suggested by the 118-point OPS dropoff. The dingers largely didn't recur, but he improved on a career-high walk rate and saw a negligible drop-off per DRC+. The glove remained versatile and per FRAA, was the most productive of Canha's career. It wasn't a step forward from 2019's breakout, but neither was it a step back—and any foodie knows if you like a dish enough the first time, you don't mind ordering it again.

YEAR	TEAM	LVL	AGE	PA	DRC+	BABIP	BRR	FRAA	WARP
2018	OAK	MLB	29	411	115	.281	-0.3	CF(62): -5.9, LF(51): 1.4, 1B(15): -0.8	1.5
2019	OAK	MLB	30	497	134	.308	1.3	CF(56): -3.8, RF(27): 1.9, 1B(15): -1.3	3.5
2020	OAK	MLB	31	243	127	.307	0.0	RF(17): 1.7, LF(15): 1.3, CF(9): 0.5	1.6
2021 FS	OAK	MLB	32	600	117	.285	-0.5	LF 4, RF 1	3.4
2021 DC	OAK	MLB	32	584	117	.285	-0.5	LF 4, RF 1	3.1

Mark Canha, continued

Batted Ball Distribution

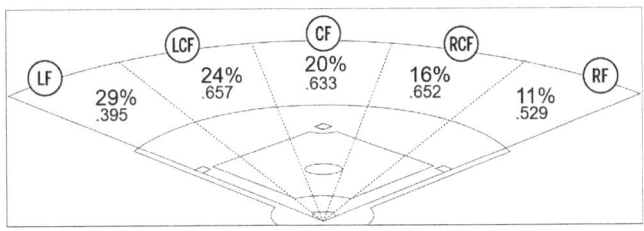

Strike Zone vs LHP

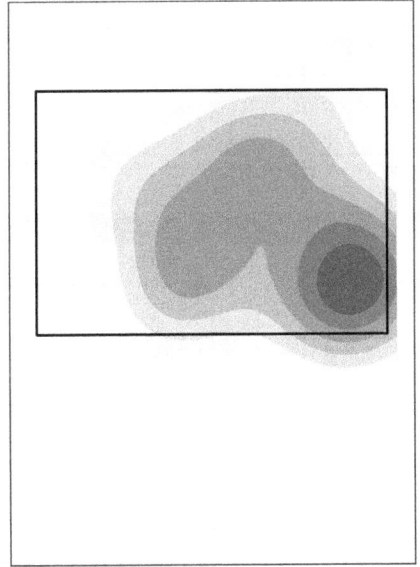

Strike Zone vs RHP

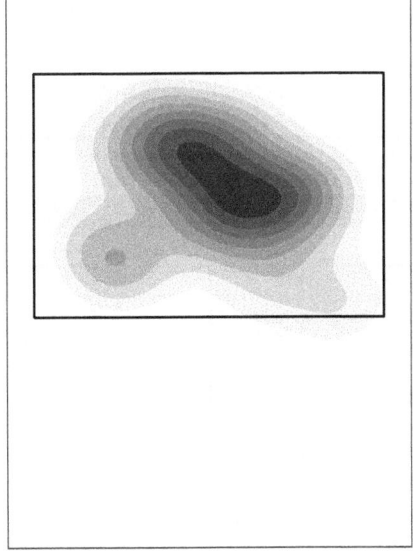

Oakland Athletics 2021

Matt Chapman 3B

Born: 04/28/93   Age: 28   Bats: R   Throws: R
Height: 6'0"   Weight: 215   Origin: Round 1, 2014 Draft (#25 overall)

YEAR	TEAM	LVL	AGE	PA	R	2B	3B	HR	RBI	BB	K	SB	CS	AVG/OBP/SLG
2018	OAK	MLB	25	616	100	42	6	24	68	58	146	1	2	.278/.356/.508
2019	OAK	MLB	26	670	102	36	3	36	91	73	146	1	1	.249/.342/.506
2020	OAK	MLB	27	152	22	9	2	10	25	8	54	0	0	.232/.276/.535
2021 FS	OAK	MLB	28	600	88	25	2	32	83	58	188	2	1	.227/.309/.469
2021 DC	OAK	MLB	28	640	94	27	3	34	89	62	201	2	1	.227/.309/.469

Comparables: Dean Palmer, J.D. Davis, Pedro Álvarez

The Hunger Games: Mockingjay; *The Godfather: Part III*; Chapman's 2020 season. We're sorry, the category was "disappointing third trilogy entries." Bothered all season by a hip injury, Chapman noted that he never felt like he had his legs under him even before a torn hip labrum in mid-September necessitated surgery and ended his worst of four campaigns. It showed at the plate, where a 35.5 percent strikeout and 5.3 percent walk rate (both career-worsts) resulted in the lowest DRC+ of his career. More worrisome, the toll was evident on the defense that had just won consecutive platinum gloves: Chapman struggled to make some basic plays and the trademark, awesome (in the original sense, heavy on "awe") arm sometimes faltered. No matter how evident it is an injury was the culprit, the seriousness of the malady ensures concern over the latent superstar will linger until he's back to gunning out runners from unfathomable distances across the diamond.

YEAR	TEAM	LVL	AGE	PA	DRC+	BABIP	BRR	FRAA	WARP
2018	OAK	MLB	25	616	125	.338	3.8	3B(145): 15.6	6.2
2019	OAK	MLB	26	670	120	.270	-3.2	3B(156): 12.9	5.2
2020	OAK	MLB	27	152	92	.291	0.3	3B(36): -5.6, SS(1): 0.0	-0.3
2021 FS	OAK	MLB	28	600	112	.281	-0.4	3B 3, SS 0	2.4
2021 DC	OAK	MLB	28	640	112	.281	-0.5	3B 4	2.5

Matt Chapman, continued

Batted Ball Distribution

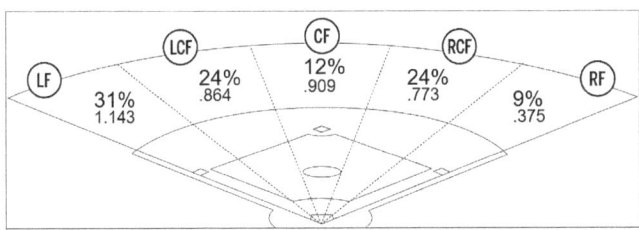

Strike Zone vs LHP

Strike Zone vs RHP

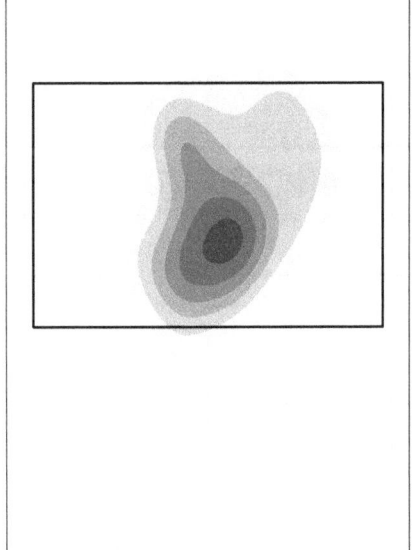

Oakland Athletics 2021

Jake Lamb 3B

Born: 10/09/90   Age: 30   Bats: L   Throws: R
Height: 6'3"   Weight: 215   Origin: Round 6, 2012 Draft (#213 overall)

YEAR	TEAM	LVL	AGE	PA	R	2B	3B	HR	RBI	BB	K	SB	CS	AVG/OBP/SLG
2018	ARI	MLB	27	238	34	8	0	6	31	26	65	1	2	.222/.307/.348
2019	RNO	AAA	28	46	5	2	0	1	7	7	12	0	0	.179/.304/.308
2019	ARI	MLB	28	226	26	8	2	6	30	32	55	1	0	.193/.323/.353
2020	OAK	MLB	29	49	5	4	0	3	9	2	8	0	0	.267/.327/.556
2020	ARI	MLB	29	50	2	1	0	0	1	6	17	0	1	.116/.240/.140
2021 FS	OAK	MLB	30	600	66	24	3	19	69	70	165	4	3	.215/.316/.390
2021 DC	OAK	MLB	30	169	18	6	0	5	19	19	46	1	1	.215/.316/.390

Comparables: Jack Howell, Ian Stewart, Mike Pagliarulo

There are no extant masks that were actually worn in Greek theater, given that they tended to be made from perishable materials such as wood or linen. Examples you might be familiar with, like the comedy and tragedy masks, are taken from paintings or terracotta simulacrums. It's theorized, though, that the comedy and tragedy masks were fashioned in the likeness of different points in Lamb's 2020 season: The first, when he was designated for assignment by the flailing D'Backs in early September with a .380 OPS; the second when he posted a mark 500 points higher as the fill-in for Matt Chapman and made the A's playoff roster. It was an almost self-parodic addition by the Oakland front office, made only more so by the fact it worked.

YEAR	TEAM	LVL	AGE	PA	DRC+	BABIP	BRR	FRAA	WARP
2018	ARI	MLB	27	238	79	.286	1.6	3B(52): -3.7	0.0
2019	RNO	AAA	28	46	70	.231	0.0	3B(6): -0.8, 1B(5): -0.0	-0.1
2019	ARI	MLB	28	226	94	.234	2.3	3B(36): -1.6, 1B(24): -1.3	0.4
2020	OAK	MLB	29	49	75	.265	0.0	3B(11): -1.9	-0.2
2020	ARI	MLB	29	50	78	.192	-0.2	1B(12): 0.2, 3B(3): 0.0	-0.1
2021 FS	OAK	MLB	30	600	96	.274	0.0	3B -2, 1B -1	0.4
2021 DC	OAK	MLB	30	169	96	.274	0.0	3B -1, 1B 0	0.1

Jake Lamb, continued

Batted Ball Distribution

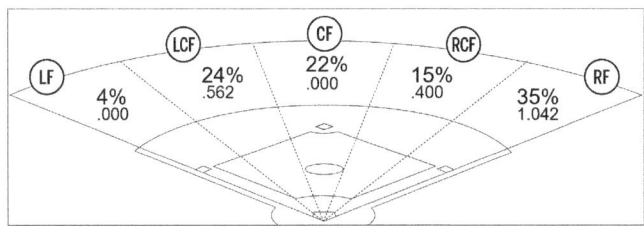

Strike Zone vs LHP   Strike Zone vs RHP

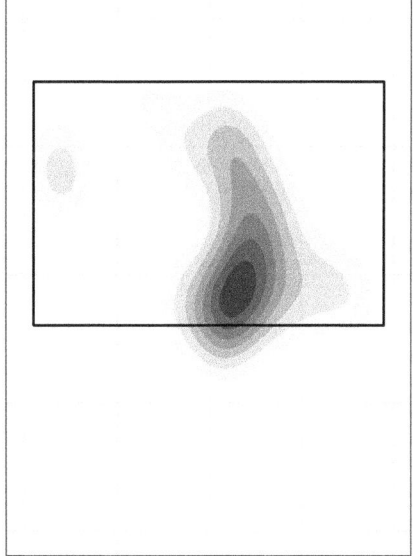

Ramón Laureano CF

Born: 07/15/94 Age: 26 Bats: R Throws: R
Height: 5'11" Weight: 203 Origin: Round 16, 2014 Draft (#466 overall)

YEAR	TEAM	LVL	AGE	PA	R	2B	3B	HR	RBI	BB	K	SB	CS	AVG/OBP/SLG
2018	NAS	AAA	23	284	44	12	1	14	35	31	70	11	2	.297/.380/.524
2018	OAK	MLB	23	176	27	12	1	5	19	16	50	7	1	.288/.358/.474
2019	OAK	MLB	24	481	79	29	0	24	67	27	123	13	2	.288/.340/.521
2020	OAK	MLB	25	222	27	8	1	6	25	24	58	2	1	.213/.338/.366
2021 FS	OAK	MLB	26	600	79	26	2	23	69	53	169	17	5	.245/.331/.437
2021 DC	OAK	MLB	26	584	77	26	2	22	67	52	165	16	5	.245/.331/.437

Comparables: Preston Wilson, Jose Cruz, Joc Pederson

Sometimes, a person comes to represent something beyond themselves. Laureano charged the Astros dugout on August 11, instigating the first bench-clearing of the 2020 season and ensuring a suspension, for the most personal of reasons: He heard Astros hitting coach Alex Cintrón say something about his mother. (Cintrón denies the maternal insult, but was suspended 20 games for saying *something* to provoke Laureano, compared to an eventual four games for the outfielder.) In a season without fans to needle the Houston players, though, Laureano's rush toward the dugout went beyond the personal for all those still feeling aggrieved by a squad that saw little reprisal. He's also established himself as one of the best defensive center fielders in baseball, adding baserunning skills to a package that's star-level even if he never takes the next step as a batter. This version of Laureano, even with a four-game suspension, was by WARP the 13th best position player in baseball.

YEAR	TEAM	LVL	AGE	PA	DRC+	BABIP	BRR	FRAA	WARP
2018	NAS	AAA	23	284	144	.358	1.7	RF(45): 6.2, CF(19): -0.5, LF(1): -0.0	2.5
2018	OAK	MLB	23	176	92	.388	1.4	CF(47): 3.0	0.9
2019	OAK	MLB	24	481	115	.342	2.2	CF(110): 9.0, RF(13): 5.1	4.2
2020	OAK	MLB	25	222	107	.270	0.8	CF(53): 8.3	1.7
2021 FS	OAK	MLB	26	600	112	.313	0.9	CF 9, LF 0	3.8
2021 DC	OAK	MLB	26	584	112	.313	0.9	CF 9	3.9

Ramón Laureano, continued

Batted Ball Distribution

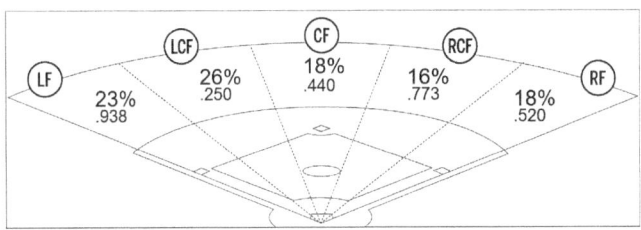

Strike Zone vs LHP   Strike Zone vs RHP

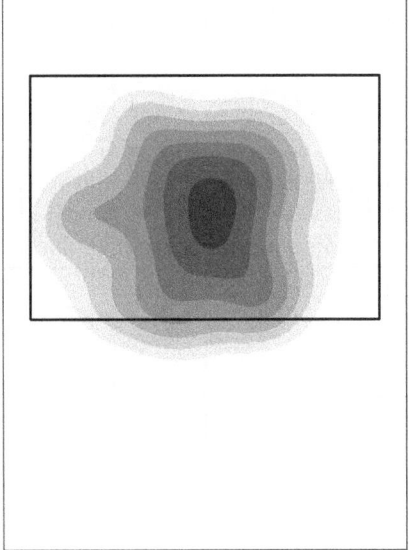

Sean Murphy C

Born: 10/04/94 Age: 26 Bats: R Throws: R
Height: 6'3" Weight: 228 Origin: Round 3, 2016 Draft (#83 overall)

YEAR	TEAM	LVL	AGE	PA	R	2B	3B	HR	RBI	BB	K	SB	CS	AVG/OBP/SLG
2018	MID	AA	23	289	51	26	2	8	43	23	47	3	0	.288/.358/.498
2019	ASGO	ROK	24	32	8	2	0	1	1	4	4	0	0	.214/.312/.393
2019	LV	AAA	24	140	25	6	1	10	30	15	31	0	1	.308/.386/.625
2019	OAK	MLB	24	60	14	5	0	4	8	6	16	0	0	.245/.333/.566
2020	OAK	MLB	25	140	21	5	0	7	14	24	37	0	0	.233/.364/.457
2021 FS	OAK	MLB	26	600	73	25	1	23	74	50	150	0	1	.230/.300/.411
2021 DC	OAK	MLB	26	371	45	15	0	14	46	31	93	0	1	.230/.300/.411

Comparables: Josmil Pinto, Geovany Soto, Bobby Estalella

YEAR	TEAM	P. COUNT	FRM RUNS	BLK RUNS	THRW RUNS	TOT RUNS
2018	NAS	422	0.0	0.0	0.0	0.0
2019	OAK	2060	-0.2	-1.2	0.0	-1.4
2019	LV	4014	1.1	0.2	-0.5	0.8
2020	OAK	5458	-1.2	0.0	-0.1	-1.3
2021	OAK	15632	-1.2	-3.7	0.3	-4.6
2021	OAK	15632	-1.2	-2.4	0.3	-3.4

It sounds like a backhanded compliment to say something or someone is good, but not in the way you'd expect. It suggests an inviting quality, but also something off-putting: It's what one might say about a tenuous, slightly opaque new technology, or hyperpop music, or Sean Murphy's rookie season. A top-five catcher in terms of DRC+ and bases on balls, Murphy impressed enough to place just off the podium in AL Rookie of the Year voting. All of which is impressive enough, considering Murphy was perceived more as a glove-first prospect with potential for some pop. There was little expectation he'd bring to the majors a judicious eye that placed him third among all catchers in on-base percentage (minimum 100 plate appearances). The glove looked more tenuous, but given hardiness that allowed him to appear in 43 games and catch every playoff inning—another reversal, given an injury-fraught path to the majors—there's enough here to profile Murphy as an average or better starter.

YEAR	TEAM	LVL	AGE	PA	DRC+	BABIP	BRR	FRAA	WARP
2018	MID	AA	23	289	133	.324	2.1	C(65): 14.5	3.4
2019	ASGO	ROK	24	32		.217			
2019	LV	AAA	24	140	122	.329	-1.3	C(27): 1.5	1.0
2019	OAK	MLB	24	60	97	.273	1.1	C(18): -1.6	0.2
2020	OAK	MLB	25	140	112	.278	-0.5	C(43): -0.2	0.7
2021 FS	OAK	MLB	26	600	97	.272	-0.9	C -6	1.5
2021 DC	OAK	MLB	26	371	97	.272	-0.5	C -5	0.8

Sean Murphy, continued

Batted Ball Distribution

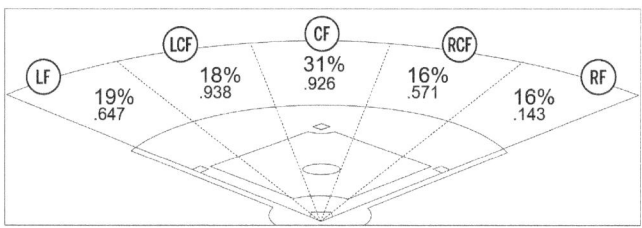

Strike Zone vs LHP   Strike Zone vs RHP

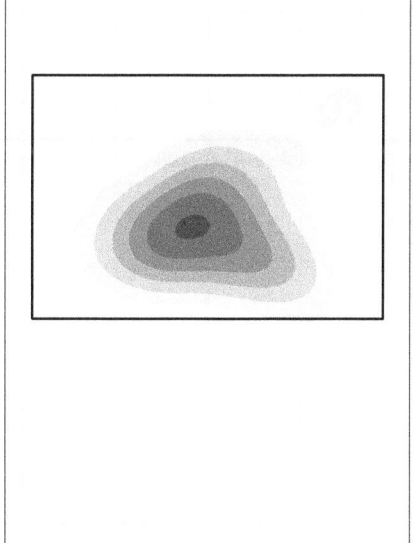

Matt Olson 1B

Born: 03/29/94 Age: 27 Bats: L Throws: R
Height: 6'5" Weight: 225 Origin: Round 1, 2012 Draft (#47 overall)

YEAR	TEAM	LVL	AGE	PA	R	2B	3B	HR	RBI	BB	K	SB	CS	AVG/OBP/SLG
2018	OAK	MLB	24	660	85	33	0	29	84	70	163	2	1	.247/.335/.453
2019	OAK	MLB	25	547	73	26	0	36	91	51	138	0	0	.267/.351/.545
2020	OAK	MLB	26	245	28	4	1	14	42	34	77	1	0	.195/.310/.424
2021 FS	OAK	MLB	27	600	89	21	1	36	86	79	181	0	1	.235/.344/.493
2021 DC	OAK	MLB	27	592	88	21	1	35	85	78	178	0	1	.235/.344/.493

Comparables: Paul Goldschmidt, Mike Napoli, Chris Carter

Defense is rarely incidental for a first baseman; what is already the least valuable position on the defensive spectrum becomes something of a self-fulfilling prophecy as players who are already slow, lack range, or have other defensive limitations are shifted down the spectrum to an eventual home at first. This to say that exemplary defense at first base is a rarity more because of incidental factors than an inherent reality of the position. Olson is the majors' preeminent example of this, following up a star-making 2019 where his 11.7 FRAA was best among primary first basemen and 21st in the majors, he was just as resplendent in the field in 2020's short season. The offense was average, a big step back, but not enough of a counterweight from the defense to drop Olson out of the top 50 position players by WARP.

YEAR	TEAM	LVL	AGE	PA	DRC+	BABIP	BRR	FRAA	WARP
2018	OAK	MLB	24	660	114	.292	-2.6	1B(162): 3.8	2.2
2019	OAK	MLB	25	547	133	.300	-1.9	1B(127): 11.7	4.1
2020	OAK	MLB	26	245	101	.227	0.3	1B(60): 4.7	1.1
2021 FS	OAK	MLB	27	600	128	.284	-0.9	1B 2	3.2
2021 DC	OAK	MLB	27	592	128	.284	-0.9	1B 2	3.1

Matt Olson, continued

Batted Ball Distribution

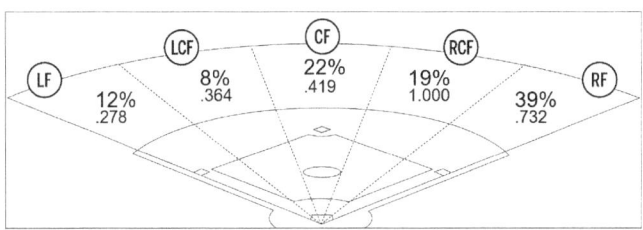

Strike Zone vs LHP   Strike Zone vs RHP

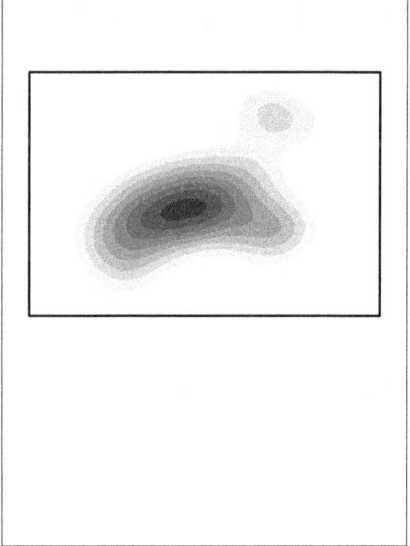

Oakland Athletics 2021

Chad Pinder 2B

Born: 03/29/92   Age: 29   Bats: R   Throws: R
Height: 6'2"   Weight: 210   Origin: Round 2, 2013 Draft (#71 overall)

YEAR	TEAM	LVL	AGE	PA	R	2B	3B	HR	RBI	BB	K	SB	CS	AVG/OBP/SLG
2018	OAK	MLB	26	333	43	12	1	13	27	27	88	0	2	.258/.332/.436
2019	OAK	MLB	27	370	45	21	0	13	47	20	88	0	1	.240/.290/.416
2020	OAK	MLB	28	61	8	3	0	2	8	5	13	0	0	.232/.295/.393
2021 FS	OAK	MLB	29	600	69	26	1	22	73	39	163	2	1	.237/.297/.414
2021 DC	OAK	MLB	29	448	51	20	1	16	55	29	122	1	1	.237/.297/.414

Comparables: Marcus Thames, Matt Luke, Pete Incaviglia

    Pinder has two definitions: the first is a word for peanut, chiefly used in the South; the second is a word for a person who impounds animals, chiefly used in the U.K. You might notice the A's Pinder doesn't get a definition, because he continued to staunchly refuse one. Appearing at "only" four positions (in contrast to seven, all but pitcher and catcher, in the previous two seasons), Pinder was right in line with his career offensive baseline, but he saw no play at shortstop and center fielder and also posted the worst FRAA of his five seasons, calling into question whether he's still a "super"-utility going forward. A bench player who can fill in at multiple positions, you want; a bench player who can be slotted in anywhere on the field, you need. Divergent definitions.

YEAR	TEAM	LVL	AGE	PA	DRC+	BABIP	BRR	FRAA	WARP
2018	OAK	MLB	26	333	109	.325	0.8	LF(64): 4.8, 2B(21): -1.3, 3B(16): 0.2	1.8
2019	OAK	MLB	27	370	81	.284	0.9	LF(46): 2.4, RF(34): 4.2, 2B(21): -2.1	0.7
2020	OAK	MLB	28	61	94	.268	-0.3	2B(13): -1.8, 3B(7): 0.4, LF(2): -0.0	0.0
2021 FS	OAK	MLB	29	600	96	.293	-0.7	2B -6, SS 0	0.5
2021 DC	OAK	MLB	29	448	96	.293	-0.6	2B -5, SS 0	0.6

Chad Pinder, continued

Batted Ball Distribution

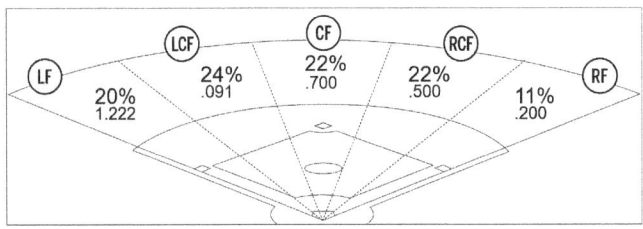

Strike Zone vs LHP   Strike Zone vs RHP

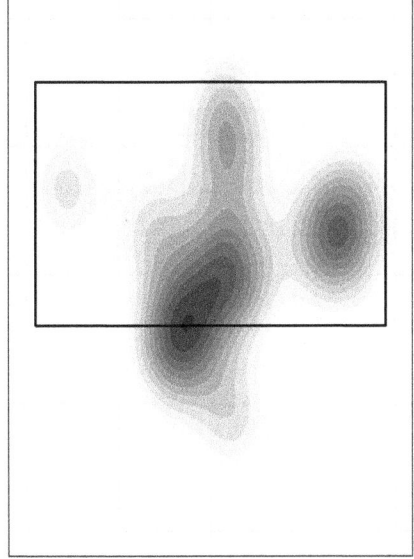

Oakland Athletics 2021

Stephen Piscotty RF
Born: 01/14/91   Age: 30   Bats: R   Throws: R
Height: 6'4"   Weight: 211   Origin: Round 1, 2012 Draft (#36 overall)

YEAR	TEAM	LVL	AGE	PA	R	2B	3B	HR	RBI	BB	K	SB	CS	AVG/OBP/SLG
2018	OAK	MLB	27	605	78	41	0	27	88	42	114	2	0	.267/.331/.491
2019	OAK	MLB	28	393	46	17	1	13	44	29	84	2	0	.249/.309/.412
2020	OAK	MLB	29	171	17	6	0	5	29	9	53	4	0	.226/.271/.358
2021 FS	OAK	MLB	30	600	71	26	1	21	73	52	160	4	3	.235/.311/.411
2021 DC	OAK	MLB	30	490	58	21	1	17	59	42	131	4	2	.235/.311/.411

Comparables: Michael Cuddyer, Mike Marshall, Ryan Church

Sometimes, everything points in the wrong direction—phone battery dwindling, frustration mounting, mental list of tasks to complete before heading home never-ending. In Piscotty's case those markers were concrete, as he posted the highest strikeout (31 percent) and lowest walk (5.3 percent) rates of his six-year career along with his worst marks in all of batting average, on-base, slugging, and isolated slugging percentages, plus DRC+. The defense has always been shaky and passable baserunning is hardly useful when you can't get on base—by WARP, Piscotty was the worst Athletic by more than half a win. Only the remaining two years of a six-year deal signed early in his career ensure Piscotty's starting role into 2021.

YEAR	TEAM	LVL	AGE	PA	DRC+	BABIP	BRR	FRAA	WARP
2018	OAK	MLB	27	605	120	.290	-1.4	RF(151): -9.3	1.7
2019	OAK	MLB	28	393	94	.289	1.1	RF(90): -3.7	0.4
2020	OAK	MLB	29	171	79	.304	0.2	RF(44): -6.9	-0.8
2021 FS	OAK	MLB	30	600	99	.292	-0.5	RF -2	1.0
2021 DC	OAK	MLB	30	490	99	.292	-0.4	RF -1	0.8

Stephen Piscotty, continued

Batted Ball Distribution

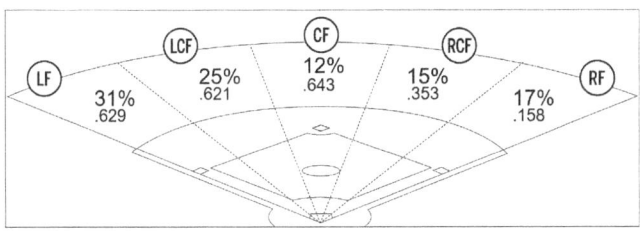

Strike Zone vs LHP   Strike Zone vs RHP

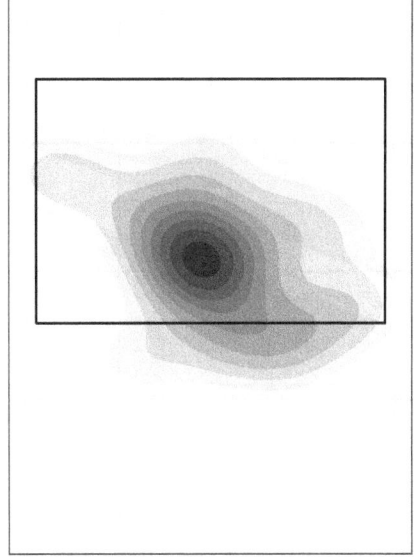

Oakland Athletics 2021

Chris Bassitt   RHP
Born: 02/22/89   Age: 32   Bats: R   Throws: R
Height: 6'5"   Weight: 217   Origin: Round 16, 2011 Draft (#501 overall)

YEAR	TEAM	LVL	AGE	W	L	SV	G	GS	IP	H	HR	BB/9	K/9	K	GB%	BABIP
2018	NAS	AAA	29	5	5	0	18	14	81²	86	6	2.8	9.1	83	42.8%	.349
2018	OAK	MLB	29	2	3	0	11	7	47²	40	4	3.6	7.7	41	43.6%	.265
2019	LV	AAA	30	0	0	0	2	2	8	8	2	2.2	10.1	9	58.3%	.273
2019	OAK	MLB	30	10	5	0	28	25	144	125	21	2.9	8.8	141	40.6%	.268
2020	OAK	MLB	31	5	2	0	11	11	63	56	6	2.4	7.9	55	43.9%	.278
2021 FS	OAK	MLB	32	9	8	0	26	26	150	142	21	3.2	8.6	142	42.9%	.288
2021 DC	OAK	MLB	32	9	8	0	25	25	142.3	135	20	3.2	8.6	135	42.9%	.288

Comparables: Trevor Cahill, Jhoulys Chacín, Kyle Gibson

It was a career year for Bassitt, who didn't flounder, and ended up as the team's best starter by both ERA and WARP. It's a less lofty perch per the advanced metrics, which saw Bassitt as slightly improved from the prior season but largely still a mid-rotation starter. Never having surpassed a 23 percent strikeout rate and lacking pinpoint command, it's unclear if Bassitt has a much higher ceiling than what he showed in a small-sample-size-boosted 2020. It was still enough to drum up an eighth-place Cy Young finish, though, and two seasons of this version of Bassitt has enough tang that, come 2021, people will take more than a flier.

YEAR	TEAM	LVL	AGE	WHIP	ERA	DRA-	WARP	MPH	FB%	WHF	CSP
2018	NAS	AAA	29	1.36	4.30	80	1.6				
2018	OAK	MLB	29	1.24	3.02	116	0.0	94.0	82.3%	17.4%	
2019	LV	AAA	30	1.25	4.50	53	0.3				
2019	OAK	MLB	30	1.19	3.81	91	2.0	95.5	78.7%	21.0%	
2020	OAK	MLB	31	1.16	2.29	86	1.0	94.6	77.5%	23.0%	
2021 FS	OAK	MLB	32	1.30	4.11	97	1.7	95.1	78.6%	21.3%	52.0%
2021 DC	OAK	MLB	32	1.30	4.11	97	1.5	95.1	78.6%	21.3%	52.0%

Chris Bassitt, continued

Pitch Shape vs LHH

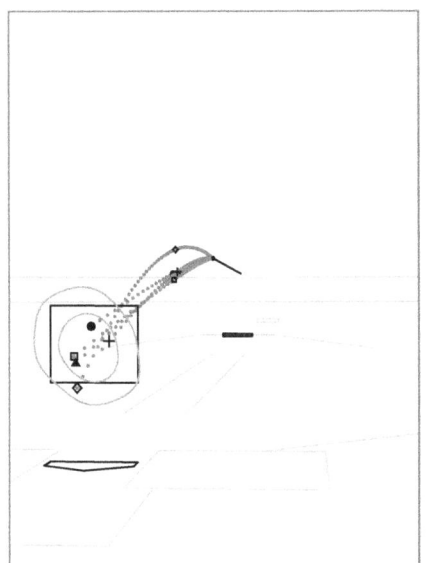

Pitch Shape vs RHH

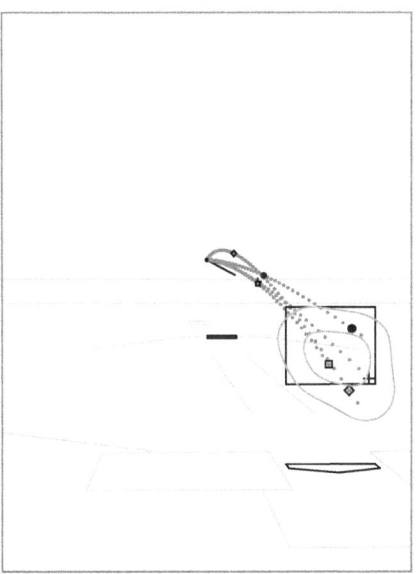

Type	Frequency	Velocity	H Movement	V Movement
● Fastball	15.8%	93.6 [103]	-6.9 [99]	-14.6 [102]
□ Sinker	38.6%	92.8 [102]	-13.9 [94]	-18.2 [108]
+ Cutter	23.2%	88 [98]	1.4 [96]	-24.3 [99]
▲ Changeup	10.3%	83.7 [94]	-15.4 [80]	-26.7 [102]
◇ Curveball	9.4%	70.2 [67]	11.1 [114]	-64.2 [65]

Oakland Athletics 2021

Jake Diekman LHP
Born: 01/21/87 Age: 34 Bats: L Throws: L
Height: 6'4" Weight: 195 Origin: Round 30, 2007 Draft (#923 overall)

YEAR	TEAM	LVL	AGE	W	L	SV	G	GS	IP	H	HR	BB/9	K/9	K	GB%	BABIP
2018	TEX	MLB	31	1	1	2	47	0	39	31	2	5.3	11.1	48	48.0%	.302
2018	ARI	MLB	31	0	1	0	24	0	14^1	18	2	5.0	11.3	18	52.4%	.400
2019	OAK	MLB	32	1	1	0	28	0	20^1	16	0	7.1	9.3	21	44.4%	.302
2019	KC	MLB	32	0	6	0	48	0	41^2	33	3	5.0	13.6	63	47.9%	.330
2020	OAK	MLB	33	2	0	0	21	0	21^1	8	1	5.1	13.1	31	60.0%	.184
2021 FS	OAK	MLB	34	2	2	7	57	0	50	39	4	5.2	11.9	66	50.0%	.299
2021 DC	OAK	MLB	34	2	2	7	58	0	60	47	5	5.2	11.9	79	50.0%	.299

Comparables: Chaz Roe, Sam Freeman, Cory Gearrin

The A's bullpen led the majors with a 2.72 ERA, which is the sort of thing that happens when a pitcher like Diekman allows just one earned run in 21 1/3 innings. The presumptive closer—and on an affordable contract, natch—showed signs of a breakout in 2019, but nothing could have predicted a 2020 in which he was nigh-unhittable. To be fair, it's hard to predict someone deciding to cop Chaz Roe's slider after seeing it on Twitter a day into the season and putting up a 19.6 percent whiff rate with it. This century, just two pitchers, 2020 Devin Williams and 2006 Matt Smith, allowed fewer than his 3.38 hits per nine innings (minimum 20 innings pitched). It's basically an impossible feat across a full season, as evidenced by none of the pitchers surpassing 30 innings. When you strike out 37 percent of batters, though, you get to break the rules a little bit. The walk rate is a ~~little~~ lot higher than you want, but again, Diekman gets to break the rules as long as he's this untouchable.

YEAR	TEAM	LVL	AGE	WHIP	ERA	DRA-	WARP	MPH	FB%	WHF	CSP
2018	TEX	MLB	31	1.38	3.69	141	-0.6	96.8	62.4%	27.5%	
2018	ARI	MLB	31	1.81	7.53	139	-0.2	97.2	67.9%	31.1%	
2019	OAK	MLB	32	1.57	4.43	98	0.1	97.3	59.1%	29.2%	
2019	KC	MLB	32	1.34	4.75	55	1.2	97.5	51.0%	38.3%	
2020	OAK	MLB	33	0.94	0.42	66	0.6	97.0	59.3%	40.8%	
2021 FS	OAK	MLB	34	1.37	3.77	87	0.6	97.2	57.4%	35.1%	47.6%
2021 DC	OAK	MLB	34	1.37	3.77	87	0.7	97.2	57.4%	35.1%	47.6%

Jake Diekman, continued

Pitch Shape vs LHH

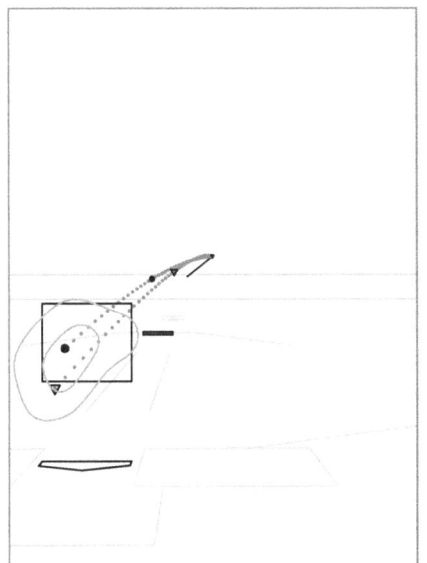

Pitch Shape vs RHH

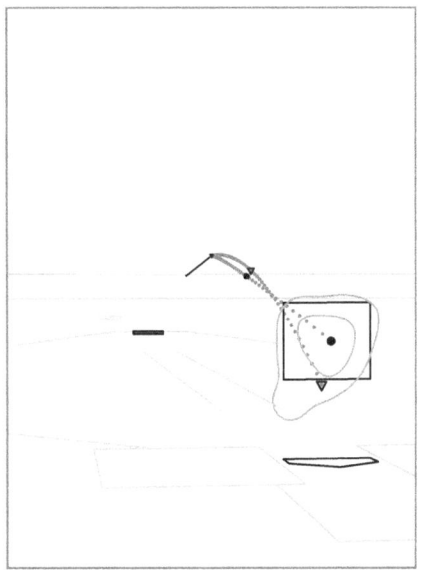

Type	Frequency	Velocity	H Movement	V Movement
● Fastball	52.0%	95.3 [109]	11.6 [77]	-15.3 [100]
☐ Sinker	6.7%	95 [113]	15.5 [82]	-19.7 [103]
▽ Slider	39.9%	82.7 [94]	-12.4 [127]	-35.6 [95]

Oakland Athletics 2021

Mike Fiers   RHP
Born: 06/15/85   Age: 36   Bats: R   Throws: R
Height: 6'2"   Weight: 211   Origin: Round 22, 2009 Draft (#676 overall)

YEAR	TEAM	LVL	AGE	W	L	SV	G	GS	IP	H	HR	BB/9	K/9	K	GB%	BABIP
2018	OAK	MLB	33	5	2	0	10	9	53	45	12	1.9	8.8	52	42.5%	.246
2018	DET	MLB	33	7	6	0	21	21	119	121	20	2.0	6.6	87	38.0%	.278
2019	OAK	MLB	34	15	4	0	33	33	184^2	166	30	2.6	6.1	126	38.9%	.256
2020	OAK	MLB	35	6	3	0	11	11	59	65	9	2.4	5.6	37	34.5%	.293
2021 FS	OAK	MLB	36	8	9	0	26	26	150	161	30	2.8	6.4	107	37.6%	.283
2021 DC	OAK	MLB	36	7	8	0	24	24	131	141	26	2.8	6.4	93	37.6%	.283

Comparables: Aníbal Sánchez, Ian Kennedy, Ted Lilly

It's hard to fathom how, exactly, Fiers might have captured the public's interest more in 2020 than in the preceding year, when he tossed the second no-hitter of his career and then, after the season, went on the record about the Astros cheating scheme, pushing the first of a series of dominoes that cost the Astros their GM and both Houston and Boston their manager (and also the Mets, because the Mets). Despite his offseason notoriety, Fiers was mostly anonymous on the field, losing two ticks off his fastball and going below replacement level, with the worst DRA on the A's, for only the second time in a 10-year career.

YEAR	TEAM	LVL	AGE	WHIP	ERA	DRA-	WARP	MPH	FB%	WHF	CSP
2018	OAK	MLB	33	1.06	3.74	89	0.8	92.0	51.2%	21.1%	
2018	DET	MLB	33	1.24	3.48	108	0.6	91.5	46.7%	19.2%	
2019	OAK	MLB	34	1.19	3.90	103	1.4	92.4	51.7%	18.3%	
2020	OAK	MLB	35	1.37	4.58	131	-0.5	89.8	44.9%	15.7%	
2021 FS	OAK	MLB	36	1.38	5.01	116	0.1	91.6	49.2%	18.0%	49.6%
2021 DC	OAK	MLB	36	1.38	5.01	116	0.1	91.6	49.2%	18.0%	49.6%

Mike Fiers, continued

Pitch Shape vs LHH

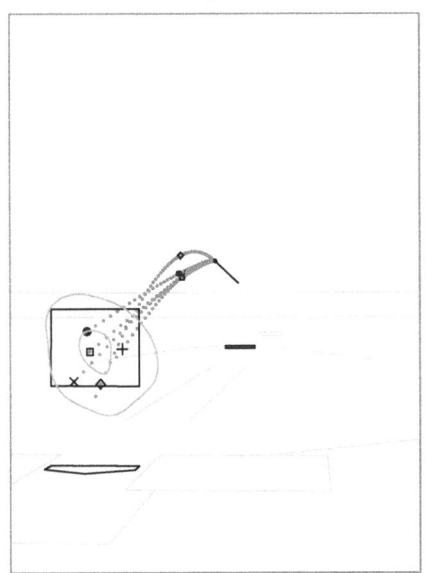

Pitch Shape vs RHH

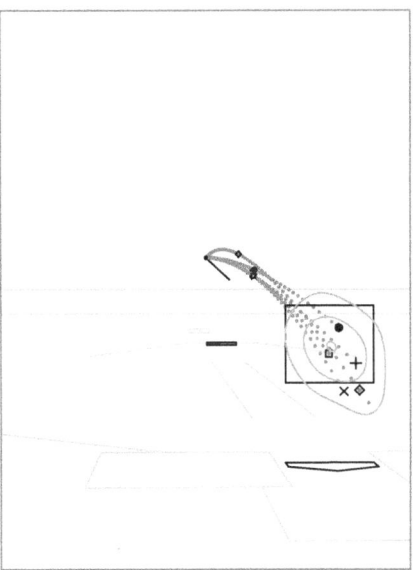

Type	Frequency	Velocity	H Movement	V Movement
● Fastball	24.0%	88.1 [86]	-8.7 [91]	-15.7 [99]
□ Sinker	20.9%	88.1 [78]	-12.2 [106]	-19.3 [104]
+ Cutter	26.9%	84.3 [75]	1 [94]	-23.9 [101]
× Splitter	16.0%	82.2 [86]	-13 [81]	-31.2 [94]
◇ Curveball	12.2%	72.8 [77]	9.6 [108]	-61.6 [71]

Adam Kolarek LHP

Born: 01/14/89 Age: 32 Bats: L Throws: L
Height: 6'3" Weight: 215 Origin: Round 11, 2010 Draft (#332 overall)

YEAR	TEAM	LVL	AGE	W	L	SV	G	GS	IP	H	HR	BB/9	K/9	K	GB%	BABIP
2018	DUR	AAA	29	5	1	4	31	1	44^2	35	1	2.4	10.5	52	60.7%	.309
2018	TB	MLB	29	1	0	2	31	0	34^1	38	0	1.3	5.0	19	57.8%	.328
2019	TB	MLB	30	4	3	1	54	0	43^1	39	6	2.9	7.5	36	63.4%	.264
2019	LAD	MLB	30	2	0	0	26	0	11^2	9	1	1.5	6.9	9	73.5%	.242
2020	LAD	MLB	31	3	0	1	20	0	19	11	1	1.9	6.2	13	61.8%	.185
2021 FS	OAK	MLB	32	2	2	0	57	0	50	47	4	3.0	7.8	43	60.7%	.290
2021 DC	OAK	MLB	32	1	1	0	38	0	48	45	4	3.0	7.8	41	60.7%	.290

Comparables: Josh Osich, Matt Grace, Brandon Workman

Side-arm sinkerballers aren't supposed to be this strapping. That's the most peculiar thing about Kolarek. Nearly everyone who throws anything like the way he does is either short or wiry. Kolarek is built like a starter, but pitches like he was born for the (dying) role of matchup bullpen lefty. In 2020, he proved he can more than withstand the implementation of the three-batter-minimum rule, and only partially because that rule has turned out to be toothless. His sinker has both elite sink and elite run, and he's getting better at spotting it with each passing year. Hitters are still trying to figure out why he's not more normal—as he saws them off.

YEAR	TEAM	LVL	AGE	WHIP	ERA	DRA-	WARP	MPH	FB%	WHF	CSP
2018	DUR	AAA	29	1.05	1.61	71	0.8				
2018	TB	MLB	29	1.25	3.93	95	0.3	92.9	63.8%	20.4%	
2019	TB	MLB	30	1.22	3.95	77	0.7	92.4	82.8%	22.3%	
2019	LAD	MLB	30	0.94	0.77	77	0.2	91.5	83.2%	32.2%	
2020	LAD	MLB	31	0.79	0.95	83	0.3	91.1	83.7%	17.8%	
2021 FS	OAK	MLB	32	1.28	3.62	89	0.6	92.0	79.7%	22.0%	47.5%
2021 DC	OAK	MLB	32	1.28	3.62	89	0.5	92.0	79.7%	22.0%	47.5%

Adam Kolarek, continued

Pitch Shape vs LHH

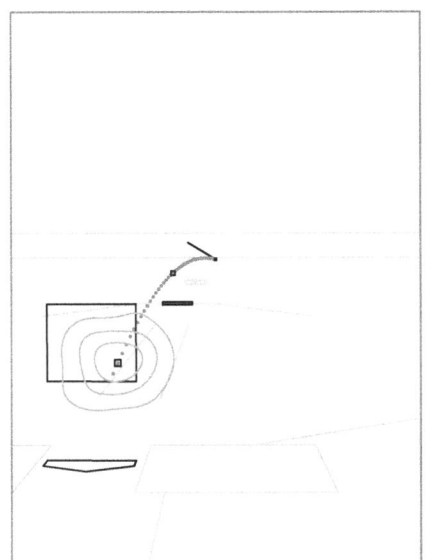

Pitch Shape vs RHH

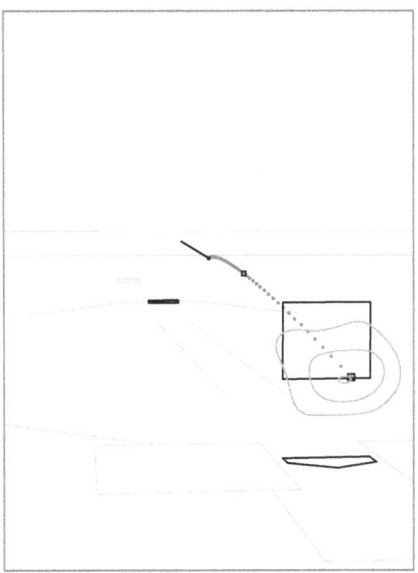

Type	Frequency	Velocity	H Movement	V Movement
● Fastball	4.0%	91.2 [96]	11 [80]	-17.7 [93]
□ Sinker	79.8%	89.1 [83]	15.2 [85]	-33.6 [58]
▲ Changeup	7.1%	81.5 [86]	16.5 [74]	-39.1 [68]
▽ Slider	9.1%	77.6 [72]	-4.4 [97]	-34 [99]

Oakland Athletics 2021

Jesús Luzardo LHP

Born: 09/30/97 Age: 23 Bats: L Throws: L
Height: 6'0" Weight: 218 Origin: Round 3, 2016 Draft (#94 overall)

YEAR	TEAM	LVL	AGE	W	L	SV	G	GS	IP	H	HR	BB/9	K/9	K	GB%	BABIP
2018	STK	HI-A	20	2	1	0	3	3	14²	6	0	3.1	15.3	25	56.0%	.240
2018	MID	AA	20	7	3	0	16	16	78²	58	5	2.1	9.8	86	44.3%	.270
2018	NAS	AAA	20	1	1	0	4	4	16	25	2	3.9	10.1	18	51.0%	.469
2019	ASGR	ROK	21	0	0	0	1	1	2	1	0	0.0	22.5	5	100.0%	.500
2019	STK	HI-A	21	1	0	0	3	1	10	6	1	0.0	16.2	18	44.4%	.312
2019	LV	AAA	21	1	1	0	7	7	31	29	3	2.3	9.9	34	55.1%	.306
2019	OAK	MLB	21	0	0	2	6	0	12	5	1	2.2	12.0	16	42.3%	.160
2020	OAK	MLB	22	3	2	0	12	9	59	58	9	2.6	9.0	59	46.2%	.308
2021 FS	OAK	MLB	23	9	8	0	26	26	150	133	19	3.7	10.0	166	46.5%	.291
2021 DC	OAK	MLB	23	8	7	0	25	25	134.7	119	17	3.7	10.0	149	46.5%	.291

Comparables: Julio Urías, José Suarez, Patrick Sandoval

With a Tommy John surgery, lat strain and shoulder strain—that's pretty much every part of the arm a pitcher might injure—all presenting roadblocks between being drafted in 2016 and his major-league debut in 2019, it's a minor victory Luzardo was simply able to hang in the rotation throughout 2020. That's the sort of thing that only gets said, though, when the results disappoint—after dominating in a short relief stint in 2019, he was merely average as he transitioned to the rotation. While he did well to avoid the injury bug, he couldn't avoid being snakebitten, racking up a 17.6 percent HR/FB ratio despite a stingy 30 percent flyball rate overall. No good comeback story ends with the hero doing just sorta okay; audiences want to see dominance, and Luzardo won't get back on the road to domination unless he can control his mechanics (and thus his exit velocities) better.

YEAR	TEAM	LVL	AGE	WHIP	ERA	DRA-	WARP	MPH	FB%	WHF	CSP
2018	STK	HI-A	20	0.75	1.23	34	0.6				
2018	MID	AA	20	0.97	2.29	69	1.8				
2018	NAS	AAA	20	2.00	7.31	61	0.5				
2019	ASGR	ROK	21	0.50	0.00						
2019	STK	HI-A	21	0.60	0.90	44	0.3				
2019	LV	AAA	21	1.19	3.19	52	1.2				
2019	OAK	MLB	21	0.67	1.50	68	0.3	98.2	48.5%	37.7%	
2020	OAK	MLB	22	1.27	4.12	93	0.8	97.6	53.3%	29.7%	
2021 FS	OAK	MLB	23	1.30	3.80	90	2.2	97.7	52.8%	30.6%	46.0%
2021 DC	OAK	MLB	23	1.30	3.80	90	1.7	97.7	52.8%	30.6%	46.0%

Jesús Luzardo, continued

Pitch Shape vs LHH

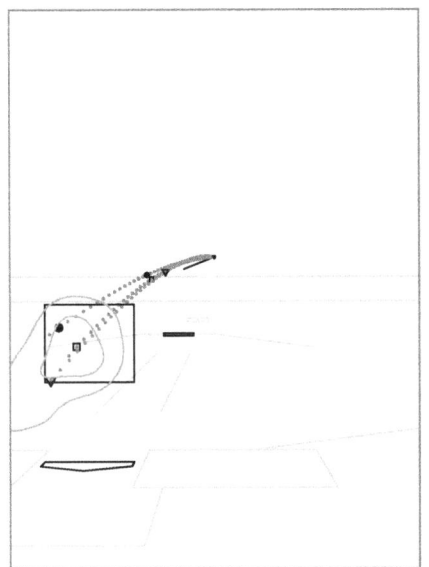

Pitch Shape vs RHH

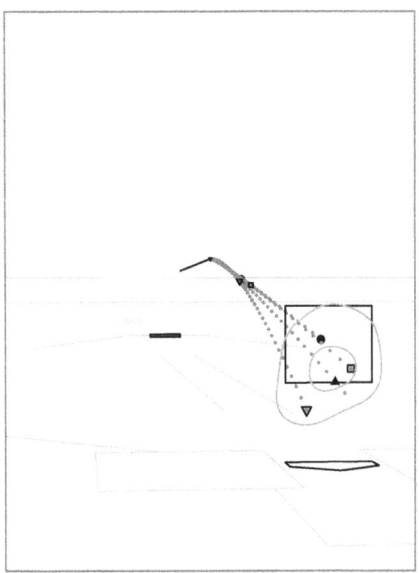

Type	Frequency	Velocity	H Movement	V Movement
● Fastball	25.3%	95.8 [110]	12.8 [71]	-14.4 [102]
□ Sinker	27.9%	95.5 [116]	15.8 [80]	-19.5 [103]
▲ Changeup	23.9%	87.5 [109]	15.3 [81]	-27.9 [99]
▽ Slider	22.7%	84.2 [101]	-1 [84]	-35.3 [96]

Sean Manaea LHP

Born: 02/01/92 Age: 29 Bats: R Throws: L
Height: 6'5" Weight: 245 Origin: Round 1, 2013 Draft (#34 overall)

YEAR	TEAM	LVL	AGE	W	L	SV	G	GS	IP	H	HR	BB/9	K/9	K	GB%	BABIP
2018	OAK	MLB	26	12	9	0	27	27	160^2	141	21	1.8	6.0	108	43.3%	.249
2019	STK	HI-A	27	0	2	0	3	3	8^1	14	1	4.3	10.8	10	42.9%	.481
2019	LV	AAA	27	3	1	0	5	5	28	16	5	1.9	13.8	43	47.3%	.224
2019	OAK	MLB	27	4	0	0	5	5	29^2	16	3	2.1	9.1	30	40.0%	.194
2020	OAK	MLB	28	4	3	0	11	11	54	57	7	1.3	7.5	45	50.0%	.311
2021 FS	OAK	MLB	29	9	8	0	26	26	150	141	22	2.4	8.9	147	46.1%	.289
2021 DC	OAK	MLB	29	9	7	0	25	25	137.3	129	20	2.4	8.9	135	46.1%	.289

Comparables: Trevor Williams, Jerad Eickhoff, José Ureña

Pokémon Black and White, the fifth generation in the highest-grossing media franchise of all time, earned some of the loftiest praise of the series for an anti-hero who asked a seemingly obvious question: "Do these pets want to fight?" Manaea, in 2020, also learned the value of asking obvious questions, when he took a 10-day layoff between August and September to ask "what if I pitched harder?" While he's still a solid three ticks below the velocity he brought to the majors, it's notable the southpaw reversed a trend of diminished velocity that had held for every season between 2015 and 2019, gaining 2.5 mph between August and October, and mixed that with an improved changeup. His results improved substantially as the season went on, and he cut his final ERA in half after it had peaked at 9.00 mid-season.

YEAR	TEAM	LVL	AGE	WHIP	ERA	DRA-	WARP	MPH	FB%	WHF	CSP
2018	OAK	MLB	26	1.08	3.59	90	2.4	92.5	56.2%	20.2%	
2019	STK	HI-A	27	2.16	9.72	192	-0.4				
2019	LV	AAA	27	0.79	3.21	25	1.5				
2019	OAK	MLB	27	0.78	1.21	82	0.6	92.5	63.5%	28.3%	
2020	OAK	MLB	28	1.20	4.50	86	0.9	92.9	54.3%	22.1%	
2021 FS	OAK	MLB	29	1.22	3.69	91	2.2	92.7	56.5%	22.3%	51.1%
2021 DC	OAK	MLB	29	1.22	3.69	91	2.0	92.7	56.5%	22.3%	51.1%

Sean Manaea, continued

Pitch Shape vs LHH

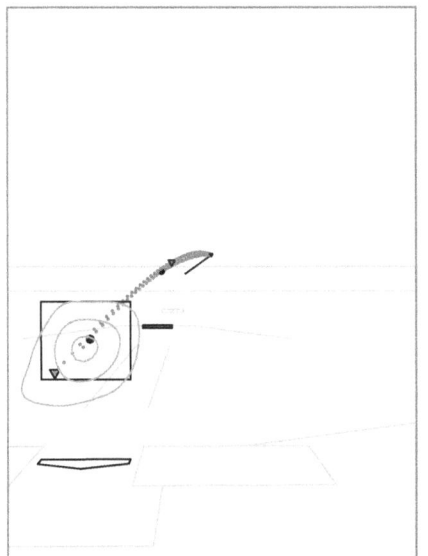

Pitch Shape vs RHH

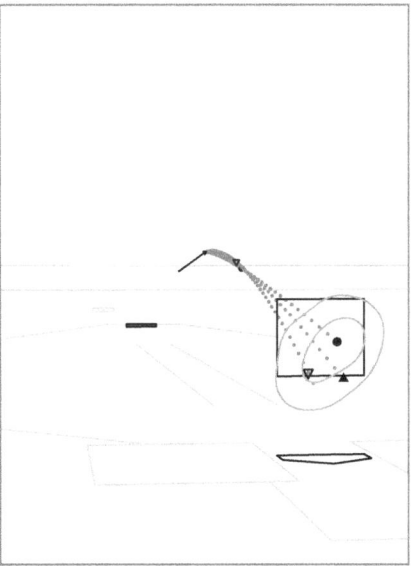

Type	Frequency	Velocity	H Movement	V Movement
● Fastball	54.3%	90.5 [93]	11.1 [79]	-20.7 [85]
▲ Changeup	28.2%	82.6 [90]	6.4 [128]	-33.9 [82]
▽ Slider	16.3%	78.9 [77]	-5.2 [100]	-39.1 [85]

Oakland Athletics 2021

T.J. McFarland LHP
Born: 06/08/89   Age: 32   Bats: L   Throws: L
Height: 6'3"   Weight: 200   Origin: Round 4, 2007 Draft (#137 overall)

YEAR	TEAM	LVL	AGE	W	L	SV	G	GS	IP	H	HR	BB/9	K/9	K	GB%	BABIP
2018	ARI	MLB	29	2	2	1	47	0	72	64	4	2.8	5.2	42	66.7%	.269
2019	ARI	MLB	30	0	0	0	51	0	56	71	6	3.2	5.6	35	59.8%	.349
2020	OAK	MLB	31	2	0	0	23	0	20^2	26	5	2.2	3.9	9	59.7%	.292
2021 FS	OAK	MLB	32	2	2	0	57	0	50	52	5	3.4	6.0	33	59.9%	.290

Comparables: Jeff Manship, Justin Grimm, Anthony Bass

Everyone's trying to recapture something. For some, it's something as simple as the feeling of youth they had in high school. Others just want the thrill of another entire conversation without saying "um" once. For T.J. McFarland, the green light is the 2018 season he finished with a 2.00 ERA and a 14 percent strikeout rate. He returned the strikeout rate in 2019 but saw the ERA more than double. Picked up by Oakland off waivers from Arizona, McFarland's 2020 was more of the same except this season featured a sub-10 percent strikeout rate, the second-worst in the majors (minimum 20 innings). You can't capture lightning in a bottle, but also McFarland might never have been lightning.

YEAR	TEAM	LVL	AGE	WHIP	ERA	DRA-	WARP	MPH	FB%	WHF	CSP
2018	ARI	MLB	29	1.19	2.00	105	0.2	91.8	72.7%	20.0%	
2019	ARI	MLB	30	1.62	4.82	134	-0.7	90.6	68.6%	22.0%	
2020	OAK	MLB	31	1.50	4.35	107	0.1	90.2	59.8%	16.3%	
2021 FS	OAK	MLB	32	1.41	4.33	102	0.2	90.8	67.4%	20.0%	41.8%

T.J. McFarland, continued

Pitch Shape vs LHH

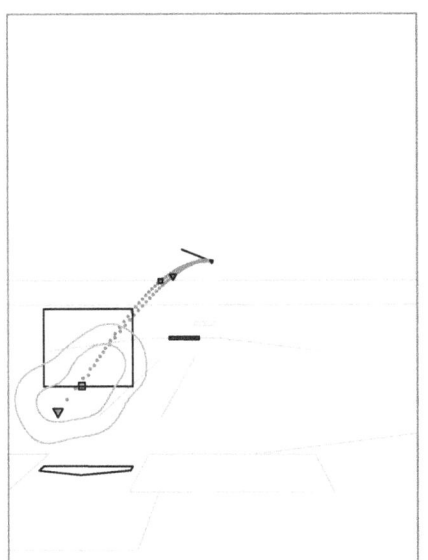

Pitch Shape vs RHH

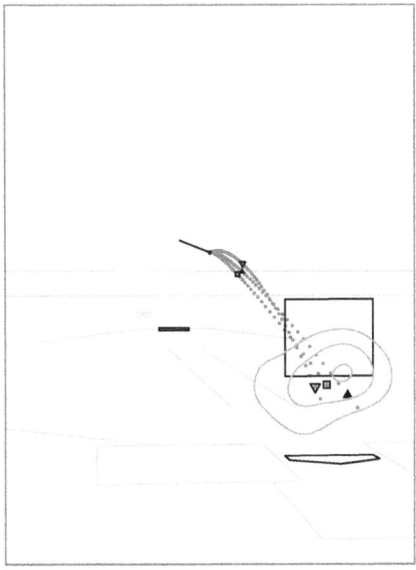

Type	Frequency	Velocity	H Movement	V Movement
☐ Sinker	59.8%	88.6 [80]	14.5 [89]	-30.5 [68]
▲ Changeup	16.6%	82 [88]	12.8 [95]	-36.1 [76]
▽ Slider	23.6%	78.4 [75]	-6.4 [104]	-42.4 [75]

Frankie Montas RHP

Born: 03/21/93   Age: 28   Bats: R   Throws: R
Height: 6'2"   Weight: 255   Origin: International Free Agent, 2009

YEAR	TEAM	LVL	AGE	W	L	SV	G	GS	IP	H	HR	BB/9	K/9	K	GB%	BABIP
2018	NAS	AAA	25	4	5	0	15	15	71²	69	7	3.3	7.7	61	46.7%	.302
2018	OAK	MLB	25	5	4	0	13	11	65	74	5	2.9	6.0	43	41.9%	.329
2019	OAK	MLB	26	9	2	0	16	16	96	84	8	2.2	9.7	103	49.6%	.297
2020	OAK	MLB	27	3	5	0	11	11	53	57	10	3.9	10.2	60	36.6%	.329
2021 FS	OAK	MLB	28	9	8	0	26	26	150	138	22	3.6	9.7	161	41.3%	.294
2021 DC	OAK	MLB	28	9	8	0	27	27	145.7	135	21	3.6	9.7	157	41.3%	.294

Comparables: Joe Musgrove, Jorge López, John Gant

In 2019, not having Frankie Montas was a big storyline for the A's in their Wild Card Game. In 2020, Montas took the win in the decisive game in the Wild Card Series—only he did it in relief. A year removed from a dominant half-season halted by a suspension for PED use, there's still lack of clarity about what sort of pitcher, exactly, Montas is. He was unilaterally worse in 2020—the K/9 went up, but that's because Montas got outs less often and highlights more a limitation of the metric than anything else; his K% slightly decreased. He walked the same number of batters as he did the previous season in 43 fewer innings. The steady decrease in velocity over the past two seasons is concerning. but even should that stabilize it'll be unclear what to make of Montas; at a certain point there's a sort of consistency in inconsistency.

YEAR	TEAM	LVL	AGE	WHIP	ERA	DRA-	WARP	MPH	FB%	WHF	CSP
2018	NAS	AAA	25	1.33	4.65	86	1.2				
2018	OAK	MLB	25	1.46	3.88	124	-0.2	97.7	72.5%	19.3%	
2019	OAK	MLB	26	1.11	2.62	64	2.7	98.4	56.8%	26.0%	
2020	OAK	MLB	27	1.51	5.60	107	0.3	97.7	62.0%	28.9%	
2021 FS	OAK	MLB	28	1.33	4.06	96	1.8	98.0	61.3%	26.2%	50.2%
2021 DC	OAK	MLB	28	1.33	4.06	96	1.7	98.0	61.3%	26.2%	50.2%

Frankie Montas, continued

Pitch Shape vs LHH

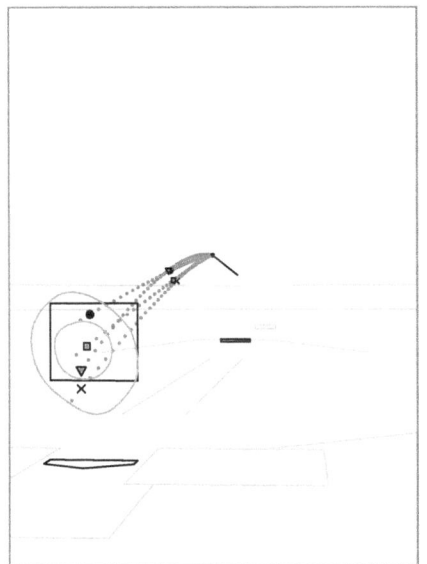

Pitch Shape vs RHH

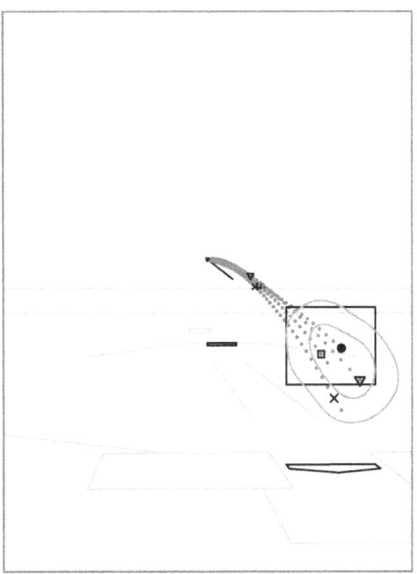

Type	Frequency	Velocity	H Movement	V Movement
● Fastball	23.9%	96 [111]	-6.7 [100]	-10.9 [112]
☐ Sinker	38.2%	95.7 [117]	-13.6 [96]	-15 [118]
✕ Splitter	12.9%	86.6 [106]	-11.2 [88]	-28.5 [103]
▽ Slider	25.1%	86.3 [110]	5.4 [101]	-31.5 [107]

Oakland Athletics 2021

Yusmeiro Petit   RHP
Born: 11/22/84   Age: 36   Bats: R   Throws: R
Height: 6'1"   Weight: 252   Origin: International Free Agent, 2001

YEAR	TEAM	LVL	AGE	W	L	SV	G	GS	IP	H	HR	BB/9	K/9	K	GB%	BABIP
2018	OAK	MLB	33	7	3	0	74	0	93	76	13	1.7	7.4	76	35.0%	.242
2019	OAK	MLB	34	5	3	0	80	0	83	57	11	1.1	7.7	71	30.0%	.214
2020	OAK	MLB	35	2	1	0	26	0	21^2	19	3	2.1	7.1	17	31.8%	.254
2021 FS	OAK	MLB	36	2	2	0	57	0	50	46	9	2.0	7.8	43	33.8%	.268
2021 DC	OAK	MLB	36	3	3	0	69	0	60	56	10	2.0	7.8	51	33.8%	.268

Comparables: Matt Belisle, Mark Melancon, Turk Farrell

Since transitioning to relief full-time in 2015, here are Petit's cFIPs: 101, 102, 86 102, 101, 105. Apart from a 2017 season in Anaheim that earned him a two-year contract with an option, even as his DRA- marks have bounced around below 100, Petit has largely been the same pitcher: someone whose stuff indicates average performance but consistently manages to turn in better results. The run prevention skill still played in 2020, but inflated walk and home run rates paired with the worst fastball velocity of his relief career portend a looming cliff. "Time's a goon, right?"

YEAR	TEAM	LVL	AGE	WHIP	ERA	DRA-	WARP	MPH	FB%	WHF	CSP
2018	OAK	MLB	33	1.01	3.00	83	1.3	91.0	47.5%	20.0%	
2019	OAK	MLB	34	0.81	2.71	80	1.3	90.6	45.8%	25.1%	
2020	OAK	MLB	35	1.11	1.66	111	0.1	89.8	42.4%	26.2%	
2021 FS	OAK	MLB	36	1.16	3.63	91	0.5	90.5	45.6%	23.9%	49.7%
2021 DC	OAK	MLB	36	1.16	3.63	91	0.6	90.5	45.6%	23.9%	49.7%

Yusmeiro Petit, continued

Pitch Shape vs LHH

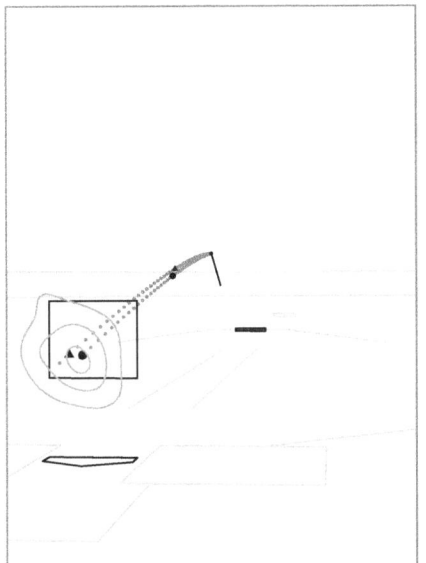

Pitch Shape vs RHH

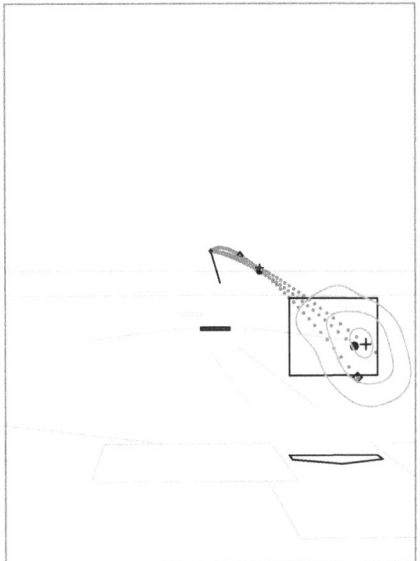

Type	Frequency	Velocity	H Movement	V Movement
● Fastball	42.2%	88.3 [86]	-4.2 [112]	-15.6 [99]
+ Cutter	28.3%	84.7 [77]	0.2 [89]	-20.4 [115]
▲ Changeup	18.1%	81.4 [85]	-8.9 [115]	-23.5 [111]
◇ Curveball	11.1%	74.6 [84]	11.6 [116]	-45.1 [107]

Oakland Athletics 2021

Burch Smith RHP
Born: 04/12/90   Age: 31   Bats: R   Throws: R
Height: 6'4"   Weight: 225   Origin: Round 14, 2011 Draft (#443 overall)

YEAR	TEAM	LVL	AGE	W	L	SV	G	GS	IP	H	HR	BB/9	K/9	K	GB%	BABIP
2018	KC	MLB	28	1	6	0	38	6	78	90	15	4.6	8.9	77	39.7%	.341
2019	SA	AAA	29	6	3	0	15	15	77^1	49	6	4.3	9.9	85	39.2%	.239
2019	SAC	AAA	29	1	1	0	3	2	15	16	1	5.4	10.8	18	51.2%	.385
2019	MIL	MLB	29	0	1	0	7	0	12^2	16	3	7.1	9.9	14	32.5%	.351
2019	SF	MLB	29	0	0	0	10	0	8^2	10	0	4.2	6.2	6	29.0%	.333
2020	OAK	MLB	30	2	0	1	6	0	12	7	1	0.8	9.8	13	30.0%	.207
2021 FS	OAK	MLB	31	2	2	0	57	0	50	45	7	4.2	9.4	52	38.1%	.284
2021 DC	OAK	MLB	31	2	2	0	47	0	30	27	4	4.2	9.4	31	38.1%	.284

Comparables: Erasmo Ramírez, Liam Hendriks, Matt Magill

In 2018, Smith was a feel-good story, re-emerging in the majors after a five-year lacuna to pitch in 38 games for Kansas City. The results were awful, leading to his ouster. In 2019 with Milwaukee, the results were again awful, leading again to his mid-season ouster. He latched on with San Francisco later that year and has since posted strong ERAs for both Bay Area squads. In 2020, he earned (per DRA) the strong results and the contract he was tendered.

YEAR	TEAM	LVL	AGE	WHIP	ERA	DRA-	WARP	MPH	FB%	WHF	CSP
2018	KC	MLB	28	1.67	6.92	140	-1.1	96.1	61.8%	24.2%	
2019	SA	AAA	29	1.11	2.33	56	2.9				
2019	SAC	AAA	29	1.67	4.20	111	0.2				
2019	MIL	MLB	29	2.05	7.82	139	-0.2	95.1	61.7%	27.7%	
2019	SF	MLB	29	1.62	2.08	170	-0.3	95.6	67.1%	17.6%	
2020	OAK	MLB	30	0.67	2.25	91	0.2	96.6	72.5%	29.1%	
2021 FS	OAK	MLB	31	1.37	4.35	101	0.2	95.9	64.2%	25.0%	49.0%
2021 DC	OAK	MLB	31	1.37	4.35	101	0.1	95.9	64.2%	25.0%	49.0%

Burch Smith, continued

Pitch Shape vs LHH

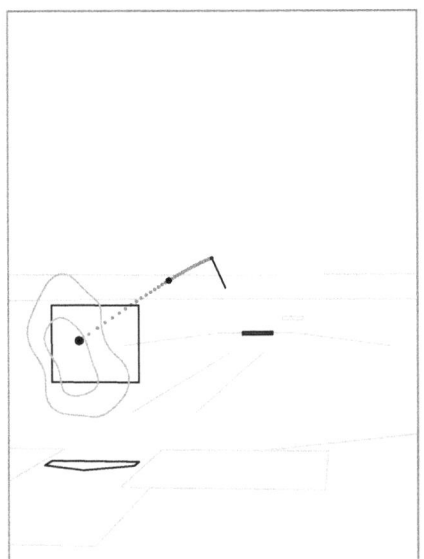

Pitch Shape vs RHH

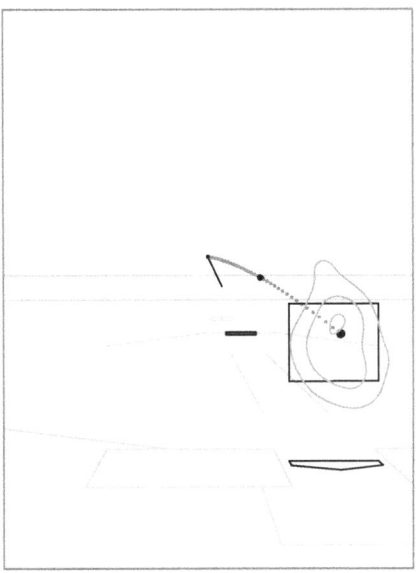

Type	Frequency	Velocity	H Movement	V Movement
● Fastball	71.9%	94.5 [106]	-7.3 [97]	-10.9 [112]
▲ Changeup	13.1%	83.1 [92]	-12.6 [95]	-23.1 [112]
◇ Curveball	14.4%	79.8 [104]	8.6 [104]	-50.9 [94]

Lou Trivino RHP

Born: 10/01/91   Age: 29   Bats: R   Throws: R
Height: 6'5"   Weight: 235   Origin: Round 11, 2013 Draft (#341 overall)

YEAR	TEAM	LVL	AGE	W	L	SV	G	GS	IP	H	HR	BB/9	K/9	K	GB%	BABIP
2018	NAS	AAA	26	0	0	1	4	0	5¹	2	0	1.7	16.9	10	37.5%	.250
2018	OAK	MLB	26	8	3	4	69	1	74	53	8	3.8	10.0	82	46.2%	.257
2019	OAK	MLB	27	4	6	0	61	0	60	61	7	4.7	8.6	57	43.8%	.320
2020	OAK	MLB	28	0	0	0	20	0	23¹	16	3	3.9	10.0	26	40.4%	.241
2021 FS	OAK	MLB	29	2	2	0	57	0	50	43	5	4.2	9.8	54	44.0%	.287
2021 DC	OAK	MLB	29	2	2	0	58	0	60	51	7	4.2	9.8	65	44.0%	.287

Comparables: Cam Bedrosian, Dominic Leone, Arodys Vizcaíno

It's not uncommon for a band's first album to be its best—The Strokes, Arcade Fire, The Velvet Underground. Sometimes, a revelatory introduction is followed up with more excellence, a declaration that this is the standard. Sometimes, you get *Room on Fire*. At that point, you have to wonder: which one was the outlier? Trivino rested on that precipice coming into 2020, following a rookie 2018 season that had him appearing as one of the league's best relievers and a 2019 that was only slightly better than indicated by the 5.25 ERA. The short season provided glimpses of how Trivino got to the peak of 2018, his K/9 again breaking double digits, but the diminished velocity and average results give little reason to expect him to again match the heights of his debut.

YEAR	TEAM	LVL	AGE	WHIP	ERA	DRA-	WARP	MPH	FB%	WHF	CSP
2018	NAS	AAA	26	0.56	1.69	27	0.2				
2018	OAK	MLB	26	1.14	2.92	69	1.6	99.2	53.7%	29.8%	
2019	OAK	MLB	27	1.53	5.25	95	0.4	98.8	50.8%	27.7%	
2020	OAK	MLB	28	1.11	3.86	91	0.3	96.8	58.8%	28.5%	
2021 FS	OAK	MLB	29	1.34	3.78	89	0.5	98.4	53.7%	28.5%	46.5%
2021 DC	OAK	MLB	29	1.34	3.78	89	0.7	98.4	53.7%	28.5%	46.5%

Lou Trivino, continued

Pitch Shape vs LHH

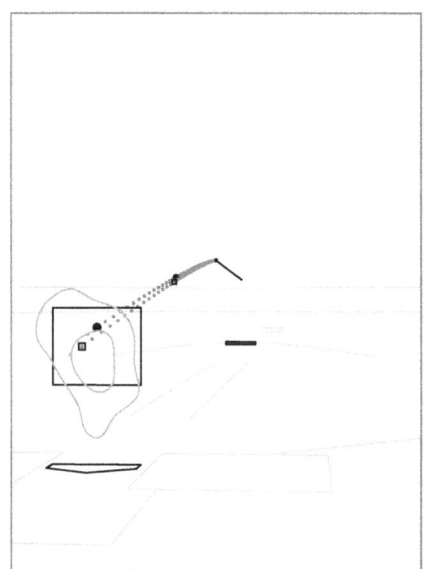

Pitch Shape vs RHH

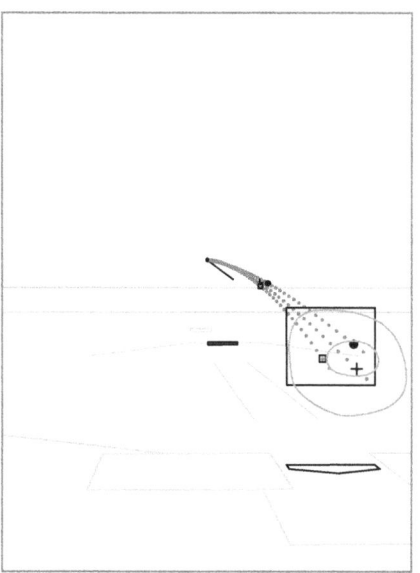

Type	Frequency	Velocity	H Movement	V Movement
● Fastball	31.4%	95.6 [109]	-7.4 [96]	-13.7 [104]
□ Sinker	27.3%	95.7 [117]	-14.2 [92]	-17.5 [110]
+ Cutter	23.2%	90.7 [115]	1.1 [94]	-24.5 [99]
▲ Changeup	7.3%	86.8 [107]	-14.6 [85]	-29.3 [95]
◇ Curveball	10.5%	78.4 [99]	11.3 [115]	-47.4 [102]

Nik Turley LHP

Born: 09/11/89 Age: 31 Bats: L Throws: L
Height: 6'4" Weight: 230 Origin: Round 50, 2008 Draft (#1502 overall)

YEAR	TEAM	LVL	AGE	W	L	SV	G	GS	IP	H	HR	BB/9	K/9	K	GB%	BABIP
2020	PIT	MLB	30	0	3	1	25	0	21^2	13	1	4.6	8.3	20	32.8%	.211
2021 FS	OAK	MLB	31	2	3	0	57	0	50	47	8	4.3	9.6	53	36.5%	.291
2021 DC	OAK	MLB	31	2	3	0	57	0	36	34	6	4.3	9.6	38	36.5%	.291

Comparables: Neil Ramírez, Matt Magill, T.J. McFarland

    A former 50th-round pick who's spent time with six different organizations plus stints in indy ball and LIDOM; significant time missed due to a PED suspension followed by TJ surgery; a three-year gap, longer than some MLB careers, between appearances in a big-league game. Turley took a circuitous journey to his first Opening Day at 30 years old, but he's more than just a feel-good story. The surface numbers don't look great but the stuff is legit: a fastball he'll spin in the top of the zone for swinging strikes and a big curve with significant two-plane break that isn't a Twitter-famous pitch yet, but should be, both for its wild movement path and the utterly hideous swings it can induce. His mound demeanor is best described as "mid-transformation werewolf doing an oral report on the Necronomicon," so proceed accordingly, gif-makers.

YEAR	TEAM	LVL	AGE	WHIP	ERA	DRA-	WARP	MPH	FB%	WHF	CSP
2020	PIT	MLB	30	1.11	4.98	111	0.1	96.1	55.5%	25.8%	
2021 FS	OAK	MLB	31	1.43	4.83	110	-0.1	96.1	55.5%	25.8%	47.1%
2021 DC	OAK	MLB	31	1.43	4.83	110	0.0	96.1	55.5%	25.8%	47.1%

Nik Turley, continued

Pitch Shape vs LHH

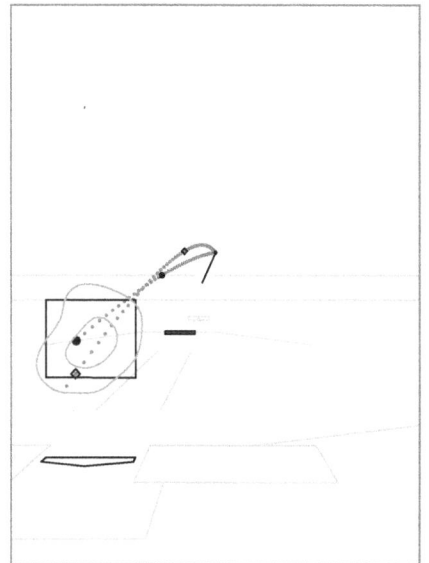

Pitch Shape vs RHH

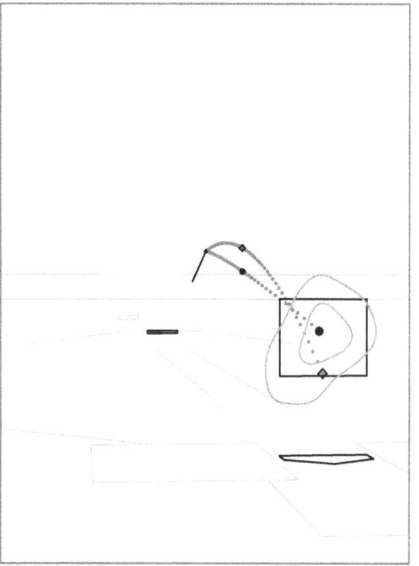

Type	Frequency	Velocity	H Movement	V Movement
● Fastball	54.9%	94.4 [106]	5.9 [104]	-13.3 [105]
◇ Curveball	44.0%	76.8 [93]	-10.9 [114]	-56.8 [81]

J.B. Wendelken   RHP

Born: 03/24/93   Age: 28   Bats: R   Throws: R
Height: 6'1"   Weight: 242   Origin: Round 13, 2012 Draft (#421 overall)

YEAR	TEAM	LVL	AGE	W	L	SV	G	GS	IP	H	HR	BB/9	K/9	K	GB%	BABIP
2018	MID	AA	25	0	1	3	11	0	13^1	11	3	6.8	15.5	23	39.3%	.333
2018	NAS	AAA	25	1	1	3	22	1	35^1	29	2	2.5	13.2	52	45.7%	.351
2018	OAK	MLB	25	0	0	0	13	0	16^2	8	1	2.7	7.6	14	39.5%	.167
2019	LV	AAA	26	6	3	3	30	1	38^2	47	8	4.4	10.0	43	46.1%	.364
2019	OAK	MLB	26	3	1	0	27	0	32^2	21	2	2.5	9.4	34	36.0%	.229
2020	OAK	MLB	27	1	1	0	21	0	25	17	2	4.0	11.2	31	46.0%	.246
2021 FS	OAK	MLB	28	2	2	0	57	0	50	40	6	3.4	10.4	57	40.2%	.273
2021 DC	OAK	MLB	28	3	2	0	58	0	48	39	6	3.4	10.4	55	40.2%	.273

Comparables: Jonathan Holder, Dovydas Neverauskas, Dan Altavilla

1 new email Subject: Try Dr. J.B. Wendelken's Intoxicating Skin Potions! Body: Re-liven your skin, with the new traditional stylings of Dr. Wendelken. Featuring new-age ingredients like 11.2 K/9 and 4.0 BB/9, you can still depend on Dr. Wendelken's for a proven combination of 95-and-a-slider and a strong ERA. It's more than just the old-timeyest name on the market; Dr. Wendelken's will emerge as a central piece of your bullpen (of skincare) when you least expect it, when your old standbys just aren't cutting it anymore. We know we're new to the market and our supply chain has been limited in past years (62 career major-league innings before 2020), but we plan to stick around. Stock up today!

YEAR	TEAM	LVL	AGE	WHIP	ERA	DRA-	WARP	MPH	FB%	WHF	CSP
2018	MID	AA	25	1.57	3.38	56	0.3				
2018	NAS	AAA	25	1.10	2.80	37	1.4				
2018	OAK	MLB	25	0.78	0.54	92	0.1	97.0	60.9%	26.8%	
2019	LV	AAA	26	1.71	5.59	115	0.2				
2019	OAK	MLB	26	0.92	3.58	84	0.4	96.4	60.6%	27.0%	
2020	OAK	MLB	27	1.12	1.80	77	0.5	96.2	58.1%	26.8%	
2021 FS	OAK	MLB	28	1.19	3.30	81	0.8	96.4	59.3%	26.9%	48.7%
2021 DC	OAK	MLB	28	1.19	3.30	81	0.7	96.4	59.3%	26.9%	48.7%

J.B. Wendelken, continued

Pitch Shape vs LHH

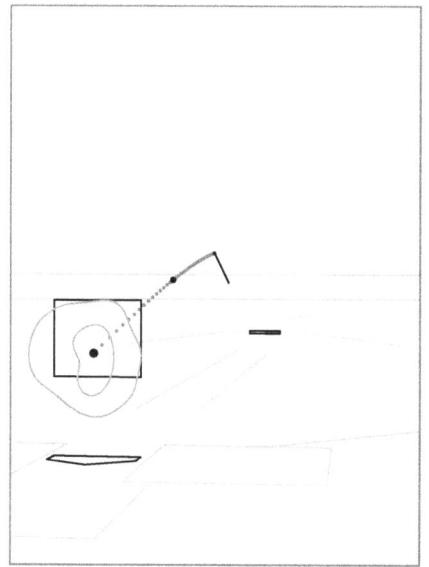

Pitch Shape vs RHH

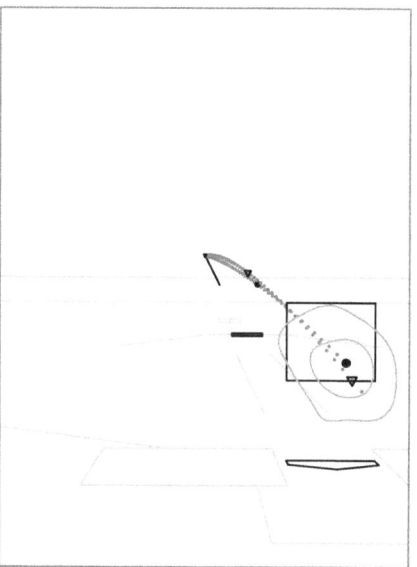

Type	Frequency	Velocity	H Movement	V Movement
● Fastball	47.1%	94.8 [107]	-2.7 [119]	-14.3 [103]
□ Sinker	11.0%	93.9 [108]	-13.6 [96]	-21.2 [98]
▲ Changeup	7.3%	86.7 [106]	-13.3 [91]	-27.8 [99]
▽ Slider	26.2%	85.5 [107]	5.7 [102]	-34 [99]
◇ Curveball	8.4%	81.1 [110]	9.4 [107]	-52.2 [92]

PLAYER COMMENTS WITHOUT GRAPHS

Austin Allen   C
Born: 01/16/94   Age: 27   Bats: L   Throws: R
Height: 6'2"   Weight: 219   Origin: Round 4, 2015 Draft (#117 overall)

YEAR	TEAM	LVL	AGE	PA	R	2B	3B	HR	RBI	BB	K	SB	CS	AVG/OBP/SLG
2018	SA	AA	24	498	59	31	0	22	56	37	97	0	3	.290/.351/.506
2019	ELP	AAA	25	298	52	27	0	21	67	22	56	0	0	.330/.379/.663
2019	SD	MLB	25	71	4	4	0	0	3	6	21	0	0	.215/.282/.277
2020	OAK	MLB	26	32	1	1	0	1	3	1	14	0	0	.194/.219/.323
2021 FS	OAK	MLB	27	600	69	21	1	24	75	38	178	0	0	.225/.281/.404
2021 DC	OAK	MLB	27	183	21	6	0	7	22	11	54	0	0	.225/.281/.404

Comparables: Yan Gomes, Ryan Doumit, Travis d'Arnaud

Allen's efficacy with the tools of ignorance has long been considered the stumbling block that might limit a plus power bat from a major-league role: After breaking 20 home runs at all of High-A, Double-A, and Triple-A (the latter in fewer than 300 plate appearances), Allen remained bogged down by both poorly regarded defense

YEAR	TEAM	P. COUNT	FRM RUNS	BLK RUNS	THRW RUNS	TOT RUNS
2018	SA	12636	8.3	1.0	3.0	12.4
2019	SD	2293	-0.1	-0.4	0.0	-0.5
2019	ELP	9133	6.9	0.0	-1.2	5.7
2020	OAK	1309	0.1	0.1	0.0	0.2
2021	OAK	6012	0.6	-0.3	-0.2	0.1
2021	OAK	6012	0.6	0.0	-0.2	0.5

and an ostentatious Padres system. Thus he found himself traded to Oakland for Jurickson Profar, whom Oakland appeared prepared to non-tender in lieu of a trade partner. After winning the backup role out of summer camp, Allen posted another sub-.600 OPS and struggled enough that he was demoted a month into the season. Behind the plate, however, Allen looked acceptable, ensuring he'll get another chance to prove his bat can translate to the bigs and serving as a reminder that just because you show someone another side of yourself, they don't have to like *that* side either.

YEAR	TEAM	LVL	AGE	PA	DRC+	BABIP	BRR	FRAA	WARP
2018	SA	AA	24	498	137	.325	-2.1	C(91): 14.6, 1B(19): -1.5	4.0
2019	ELP	AAA	25	298	128	.345	-2.5	C(61): 7.2, 1B(2): -0.1	2.8
2019	SD	MLB	25	71	61	.318	0.0	C(19): -0.2, 1B(2): 0.1	0.0
2020	OAK	MLB	26	32	68	.312	-0.3	C(14): 0.0	-0.1
2021 FS	OAK	MLB	27	600	84	.283	-1.0	C 1, 1B 0	1.1
2021 DC	OAK	MLB	27	183	84	.283	-0.3	C 0	0.4

Nick Allen SS

Born: 10/08/98 Age: 22 Bats: R Throws: R
Height: 5'8" Weight: 166 Origin: Round 3, 2017 Draft (#81 overall)

YEAR	TEAM	LVL	AGE	PA	R	2B	3B	HR	RBI	BB	K	SB	CS	AVG/OBP/SLG
2018	BEL	LO-A	19	512	51	17	6	0	34	34	85	24	8	.239/.301/.302
2019	STK	HI-A	20	328	45	22	5	3	25	28	52	13	5	.292/.362/.434
2021 FS	OAK	MLB	22	600	59	24	3	6	50	36	152	11	6	.214/.268/.306
2021 DC	OAK	MLB	22	34	3	1	0	0	2	2	8	0	1	.214/.268/.306

Comparables: José Rondón, Amed Rosario, Sergio Alcántara

Though you might not know it from looking at Oakland's system, teams are allowed to have position player prospects who impress on both offense and defense. In fairness to Allen, he tantalized with the bat in High-A during the 2019 season, but make no mistake: the glove is the carrying tool. A season of reps might have clarified if a league-average offensive baseline is a feasible expectation for the 21-year-old, might even have allowed him to step in as Marcus Semien's replacement when he inevitably leaves for less-green greener pastures, but even if the bat renders the profile more (pre-2020) José Iglesias than Andrelton Simmons, Oakland will find a way to utilize Allen and solve one of their longest-running inefficiencies: no lineup options that feature two players with the same last name (so as to confuse opposing managers).

YEAR	TEAM	LVL	AGE	PA	DRC+	BABIP	BRR	FRAA	WARP
2018	BEL	LO-A	19	512	75	.289	3.7	SS(121): 5.2	1.1
2019	STK	HI-A	20	328	134	.348	-4.4	SS(45): 4.7, 2B(24): -1.6	2.1
2021 FS	OAK	MLB	22	600	59	.281	0.9	SS 6, 2B 0	-0.7
2021 DC	OAK	MLB	22	34	59	.281	0.1	SS 0	0.0

Austin Beck OF

Born: 11/21/98 Age: 22 Bats: R Throws: R
Height: 6'1" Weight: 200 Origin: Round 1, 2017 Draft (#6 overall)

YEAR	TEAM	LVL	AGE	PA	R	2B	3B	HR	RBI	BB	K	SB	CS	AVG/OBP/SLG
2018	BEL	LO-A	19	534	58	29	4	2	60	30	117	8	6	.296/.335/.383
2019	STK	HI-A	20	367	40	22	4	8	49	24	126	2	2	.251/.302/.411
2021 FS	OAK	MLB	22	600	44	22	3	8	48	38	224	3	2	.191/.247/.285

Comparables: Yorman Rodriguez, Mickey Moniak, Willy García

Selected sixth-overall in 2017, Beck has yet to pass the *Morning Phase* of his career; being left off Oakland's 60-man player pool deprived him of much-needed time to improve at the plate and highlighted just how far the team perceives the outfielder to be from contributing at the major-league level.

Oakland Athletics 2021

YEAR	TEAM	LVL	AGE	PA	DRC+	BABIP	BRR	FRAA	WARP
2018	BEL	LO-A	19	534	105	.377	-4.8	CF(113): 2.0	0.9
2019	STK	HI-A	20	367	92	.372	-0.1	CF(69): -0.3, RF(10): 2.7	1.1
2021 FS	OAK	MLB	22	600	44	.303	-0.2	CF 4, RF 1	-1.9

Skye Bolt RF
Born: 01/15/94   Age: 27   Bats: S   Throws: R
Height: 6'2"   Weight: 180   Origin: Round 4, 2015 Draft (#128 overall)

YEAR	TEAM	LVL	AGE	PA	R	2B	3B	HR	RBI	BB	K	SB	CS	AVG/OBP/SLG
2018	STK	HI-A	24	209	28	8	4	9	32	31	47	9	3	.266/.382/.521
2018	MID	AA	24	315	41	18	3	10	37	27	75	10	1	.256/.325/.446
2019	LV	AAA	25	347	57	19	3	11	61	37	94	7	5	.269/.350/.459
2019	OAK	MLB	25	11	1	1	0	0	0	1	3	0	0	.100/.182/.200
2021 FS	OAK	MLB	27	600	64	22	2	17	64	50	195	4	3	.199/.271/.350
2021 DC	OAK	MLB	27	93	9	3	0	2	10	7	30	0	1	.199/.271/.350

Comparables: Jai Miller, Brad Snyder, Brent Clevlen

The 2008 film *Bolt* features an eponymous dog who stars in a television show in which he has superpowers; the narrative of the film concerns the dog becoming lost and learning he does not actually have superpowers. Drafted for big tools that have never quite come together as hoped, perhaps Bolt would be bolstered by the film's conclusion, when the dog learns the power of leaning into the strengths one does possess.

YEAR	TEAM	LVL	AGE	PA	DRC+	BABIP	BRR	FRAA	WARP
2018	STK	HI-A	24	209	137	.308	2.1	CF(45): -8.1, LF(4): -0.6	0.2
2018	MID	AA	24	315	104	.315	1.7	CF(50): -3.1, RF(19): 0.8	0.2
2019	LV	AAA	25	347	81	.351	-0.3	RF(40): 8.5, CF(37): 1.1, LF(7): 0.8	1.1
2019	OAK	MLB	25	11	76	.143	-0.1	CF(3): 0.0, RF(1): 0.0	0.0
2021 FS	OAK	MLB	27	600	71	.271	0.0	CF 0, RF 4	0.4
2021 DC	OAK	MLB	27	93	71	.271	0.0	CF 0, RF 1	0.0

Seth Brown OF
Born: 07/13/92   Age: 28   Bats: L   Throws: L
Height: 6'1"   Weight: 223   Origin: Round 19, 2015 Draft (#578 overall)

YEAR	TEAM	LVL	AGE	PA	R	2B	3B	HR	RBI	BB	K	SB	CS	AVG/OBP/SLG
2018	MID	AA	25	555	66	38	3	14	90	47	142	5	0	.283/.342/.454
2019	LV	AAA	26	500	101	29	6	37	104	38	127	8	1	.297/.352/.634
2019	OAK	MLB	26	83	11	8	2	0	13	7	23	1	0	.293/.361/.453
2020	OAK	MLB	27	5	0	0	0	0	0	0	2	0	0	.000/.000/.000
2021 FS	OAK	MLB	28	600	66	26	3	21	73	42	192	0	1	.223/.282/.400
2021 DC	OAK	MLB	28	231	25	10	1	8	28	16	74	0	0	.223/.282/.400

Comparables: Ben Paulsen, Joe Koshansky, Rhyne Hughes

Progressing steadily through Oakland's system after being selected in the 19th round, and hitting solidly at every stop, Brown will be feeling more like Charlie if he doesn't get a sustained shot at the majors this year.

YEAR	TEAM	LVL	AGE	PA	DRC+	BABIP	BRR	FRAA	WARP
2018	MID	AA	25	555	110	.365	1.3	1B(115): -3.7, RF(8): 4.7, LF(4): -0.2	0.2
2019	LV	AAA	26	500	112	.330	-0.2	1B(64): 0.6, LF(17): 1.0, RF(9): -0.8	1.6
2019	OAK	MLB	26	83	82	.423	1.0	LF(23): 0.3, 1B(4): -0.7	0.1
2020	OAK	MLB	27	5	74	.000		1B(3): 0.0	0.0
2021 FS	OAK	MLB	28	600	82	.299	-0.5	LF 0, 1B 0	-0.4
2021 DC	OAK	MLB	28	231	82	.299	-0.2	LF 0	0.0

Logan Davidson SS

Born: 12/26/97   Age: 23   Bats: S   Throws: R
Height: 6'3"   Weight: 185   Origin: Round 1, 2019 Draft (#29 overall)

YEAR	TEAM	LVL	AGE	PA	R	2B	3B	HR	RBI	BB	K	SB	CS	AVG/OBP/SLG
2019	VER	SS	21	238	42	7	0	4	12	31	55	5	0	.239/.345/.332
2021 FS	OAK	MLB	23	600	48	21	1	10	52	40	198	3	1	.198/.258/.302

Comparables: Yamaico Navarro, Andy Parrino, David Adams

The A's have more shortstop prospects than their stadium has problems, but Davidson could become the best of the bunch, if the 2019 first-rounder's hit tool ultimately translates as well as the arm, glove, speed, and raw power have so far.

YEAR	TEAM	LVL	AGE	PA	DRC+	BABIP	BRR	FRAA	WARP
2019	VER	SS	21	238	132	.308	1.5	SS(50): 11.8	3.0
2021 FS	OAK	MLB	23	600	56	.288	-0.4	SS 17	0.1

Oakland Athletics 2021

Greg Deichmann RF
Born: 05/31/95   Age: 26   Bats: L   Throws: R
Height: 6'2"   Weight: 205   Origin: Round 2, 2017 Draft (#43 overall)

YEAR	TEAM	LVL	AGE	PA	R	2B	3B	HR	RBI	BB	K	SB	CS	AVG/OBP/SLG
2018	ASGR	ROK	23	43	9	2	2	1	7	5	8	0	0	.289/.372/.526
2018	STK	HI-A	23	185	18	14	0	6	21	17	63	0	1	.199/.276/.392
2019	MID	AA	24	340	42	10	2	11	36	34	103	19	5	.219/.300/.375
2021 FS	OAK	MLB	26	600	65	22	3	16	59	47	216	9	3	.191/.260/.336
2021 DC	OAK	MLB	26	34	3	1	0	0	3	2	12	0	0	.191/.260/.336

Comparables: Sam Hilliard, Roger Kieschnick, Aristides Aquino

Deichmann sort of needed the 2020 season to be the one in which he pulled it all together, being a 25-year-old corner outfielder who had never posted a .700 OPS above Low-A ball. A lot of people didn't get what they wanted in 2020, though, and the A's clearly see something in the LSU product, being that they put him on the 40-man over the winter.

YEAR	TEAM	LVL	AGE	PA	DRC+	BABIP	BRR	FRAA	WARP
2018	ASGR	ROK	23	43		.345			
2018	STK	HI-A	23	185	65	.276	-0.1	RF(28): 0.7, LF(8): -0.8, 1B(5): -0.1	-0.8
2019	MID	AA	24	340	91	.289	2.7	RF(69): -0.0, CF(3): 0.2	0.7
2021 FS	OAK	MLB	26	600	63	.279	0.7	1B 0, LF 0	-1.5
2021 DC	OAK	MLB	26	34	63	.279	0.0		-0.1

Dustin Fowler CF
Born: 12/29/94   Age: 26   Bats: L   Throws: L
Height: 6'0"   Weight: 198   Origin: Round 18, 2013 Draft (#554 overall)

YEAR	TEAM	LVL	AGE	PA	R	2B	3B	HR	RBI	BB	K	SB	CS	AVG/OBP/SLG
2018	NAS	AAA	23	238	37	17	6	4	27	9	40	13	2	.342/.366/.522
2018	OAK	MLB	23	203	19	3	2	6	23	8	47	6	4	.224/.256/.354
2019	LV	AAA	24	606	98	22	7	25	89	42	145	12	4	.277/.333/.477
2021 FS	OAK	MLB	26	600	68	26	6	20	70	29	153	9	4	.243/.285/.418

Comparables: Jason Pridie, Curtis Granderson, Jake Cave

Fowler hasn't appeared in the majors since 2018, when he appeared much diminished after knee surgery the previous year. That he remains on Oakland's roster at all indicates plans for future usage, or at least an unwillingness to give up on the top prospect netted in the Sonny Gray trade, though it's unclear where Fowler will find time in a crowded outfield.

YEAR	TEAM	LVL	AGE	PA	DRC+	BABIP	BRR	FRAA	WARP
2018	NAS	AAA	23	238	121	.400	0.2	CF(51): -12.9, LF(2): 0.6	-0.1
2018	OAK	MLB	23	203	84	.262	-1.0	CF(57): -3.8, LF(3): -0.2, RF(3): -0.1	-0.2
2019	LV	AAA	24	606	81	.332	0.8	CF(89): -3.5, RF(30): 1.3, LF(6): -0.5	0.5
2021 FS	OAK	MLB	26	600	88	.298	1.1	CF -3, RF 0	0.7

Tony Kemp 2B

Born: 10/31/91   Age: 29   Bats: L   Throws: R
Height: 5'6"   Weight: 160   Origin: Round 5, 2013 Draft (#137 overall)

YEAR	TEAM	LVL	AGE	PA	R	2B	3B	HR	RBI	BB	K	SB	CS	AVG/OBP/SLG
2018	FRE	AAA	26	183	33	6	5	0	19	19	15	13	2	.335/.407/.435
2018	HOU	MLB	26	295	37	15	0	6	30	32	44	9	3	.263/.351/.392
2019	HOU	MLB	27	186	23	6	2	7	17	16	29	4	3	.227/.308/.417
2019	CHC	MLB	27	93	8	3	2	1	12	7	18	0	1	.183/.258/.305
2020	OAK	MLB	28	114	15	5	0	0	4	15	14	3	1	.247/.363/.301
2021 FS	OAK	MLB	29	600	71	27	5	12	58	59	99	10	4	.253/.336/.391
2021 DC	OAK	MLB	29	316	37	14	2	6	30	31	52	5	2	.253/.336/.391

Comparables: Tommy Harper, Mike Huff, Mike Lum

The first in a cadre of A's second basemen that never netted Oakland their second baseman of the future, Kemp moved back to the AL West in an offseason trade from Chicago and failed to thrive in the first starting role he's had in his career. Even if you're amenable to DRC+'s suggestion he was better than his dire slugging percentage suggests, the defense was also rough, and the combination disappointing enough that Oakland went with an outside hire in Tommy La Stella's trade deadline acquisition. If your employer brought in someone with your same skills and started handing them your responsibilities, you'd probably read the tea leaves. It wasn't a disastrous enough season for Kemp to be non-tendered, but you get the sense there's little hope on the team's end for a breakout or a starting role.

YEAR	TEAM	LVL	AGE	PA	DRC+	BABIP	BRR	FRAA	WARP
2018	FRE	AAA	26	183	110	.367	3.5	2B(25): -0.5, CF(14): -1.4	0.7
2018	HOU	MLB	26	295	105	.296	-0.5	LF(61): -2.8, CF(32): 0.3, 2B(7): 0.0	0.7
2019	HOU	MLB	27	186	99	.233	-1.1	2B(29): -0.9, LF(14): 0.7, CF(11): 0.1	0.4
2019	CHC	MLB	27	93	66	.215	0.8	2B(14): 0.0, LF(6): 0.5, RF(3): 0.1	0.0
2020	OAK	MLB	28	114	106	.284	0.4	2B(43): -2.1, LF(3): -0.1	0.3
2021 FS	OAK	MLB	29	600	102	.291	0.6	2B -1, LF 0	1.9
2021 DC	OAK	MLB	29	316	102	.291	0.3	2B 0, LF 0	1.0

Oakland Athletics 2021

Jed Lowrie SS

Born: 04/17/84 Age: 37 Bats: S Throws: R
Height: 6'0" Weight: 180 Origin: Round 1, 2005 Draft (#45 overall)

YEAR	TEAM	LVL	AGE	PA	R	2B	3B	HR	RBI	BB	K	SB	CS	AVG/OBP/SLG
2018	OAK	MLB	34	680	78	37	1	23	99	78	128	0	0	.267/.353/.448
2019	SYR	AAA	35	48	7	1	0	2	3	4	12	0	0	.250/.312/.409
2019	NYM	MLB	35	8	0	0	0	0	0	1	4	0	0	.000/.125/.000
2021 FS	OAK	MLB	37	600	64	25	1	17	66	60	133	0	1	.239/.320/.386

Comparables: Miguel Tejada, Rich Aurilia, Jhonny Peralta

For the second consecutive season, Jed Lowrie teased the Mets with the possibility of bringing his potent bat into the lineup, only to have an injury claim his season. This time, it was his balky left knee that brought a new injury term, "*PCL laxity*", into the Mets' increasingly robust medical lexicon.

YEAR	TEAM	LVL	AGE	PA	DRC+	BABIP	BRR	FRAA	WARP
2018	OAK	MLB	34	680	125	.304	-3.0	2B(136): -0.4, 3B(14): -0.5	3.9
2019	SYR	AAA	35	48	92	.300	0.5	2B(5): -0.5, 3B(5): -0.9, SS(1): -0.1	0.0
2019	NYM	MLB	35	8	70	.000	0.1		0.0
2021 FS	OAK	MLB	37	600	93	.288	-1.0	2B -2, 3B -1	0.8

Vimael Machín 2B

Born: 09/25/93   Age: 27   Bats: L   Throws: R
Height: 5'11"   Weight: 185   Origin: Round 10, 2015 Draft (#293 overall)

YEAR	TEAM	LVL	AGE	PA	R	2B	3B	HR	RBI	BB	K	SB	CS	AVG/OBP/SLG
2018	MB	HI-A	24	141	20	6	0	2	14	28	23	1	0	.209/.369/.318
2018	TNS	AA	24	296	30	10	1	5	28	39	54	2	1	.220/.330/.328
2019	TNS	AA	25	498	47	26	1	6	61	63	57	8	2	.294/.386/.403
2019	IOW	AAA	25	31	7	1	1	1	4	6	5	0	0	.320/.452/.560
2020	OAK	MLB	26	71	11	2	0	0	0	8	10	0	0	.206/.296/.238
2021 FS	OAK	MLB	27	600	67	25	1	12	59	63	122	0	1	.235/.321/.362
2021 DC	OAK	MLB	27	121	13	5	0	2	12	12	24	0	0	.235/.321/.362

Comparables: Eric Young Jr., Nate Spears, Sherman Johnson

The Rays might have copped the A's reputation as the most ruthless, astute pursuants of the temptress Efficiency, but the Rule 5 Draft is perhaps MLB's foremost arena where a front office can make something out of nothing, and Machin's pick-up from the Cubs was a savvy move. At 27, it's probably unrealistic to expect much further development from Machin, and in that way the pick goes against the recent grain of young, highly unpolished Rule 5 draftees. Appearing at all four infield positions and demonstrating solid pitch selection—he struck out just two times more than he walked with Oakland, and twice in the minors posted a better walk than strikeout rate—Machin figures to have set himself up to fill a utility role in the immediate future.

YEAR	TEAM	LVL	AGE	PA	DRC+	BABIP	BRR	FRAA	WARP
2018	MB	HI-A	24	141	124	.241	0.0	2B(17): 0.1, 3B(10): -0.1	0.4
2018	TNS	AA	24	296	88	.259	-2.2	2B(35): -4.5, 1B(12): -1.3, 3B(12): -0.5	-1.1
2019	TNS	AA	25	498	145	.322	-1.5	SS(47): -3.9, 2B(44): 2.8, 3B(26): -0.4	3.7
2019	IOW	AAA	25	31	119	.368	-0.9	1B(5): -0.9, 2B(3): -0.1, 3B(3): -0.1	0.0
2020	OAK	MLB	26	71	92	.245	1.0	3B(10): -0.4, SS(6): 1.1, 2B(3): -0.3	0.2
2021 FS	OAK	MLB	27	600	90	.283	-0.8	2B -1, SS -1	0.1
2021 DC	OAK	MLB	27	121	90	.283	-0.2	2B 0, SS 0	0.1

Robert Puason SS

Born: 09/11/02   Age: 18   Bats: S   Throws: R
Height: 6'3"   Weight: 165   Origin: International Free Agent, 2019

The Dominican-born Puason keeps a list of the people who helped him—and those who declined to do so. Given how quickly the shortstop, ultimately signed by the A's for $5.1 million in 2019 following a failed verbal agreement with Atlanta, has jumped up prospect lists, you wouldn't want to be on his bad list.

Oakland Athletics 2021

Tyler Soderstrom C
Born: 11/24/01 Age: 19 Bats: L Throws: R
Height: 6'2" Weight: 200 Origin: Round 1, 2020 Draft (#26 overall)

Expected to go well before the 26th pick in the first round, the A's went well over-slot to coax Soderstrom from his commitment to UCLA and wasted no time in kickstarting his development, adding him to their 60-player pool. Oakland is continuing to develop him at catcher, but the pure hitting talent and raw power are what made their executives so gleeful he fell to them. (Presumably also happy for the bragging rights is father Steve, picked 20 spots ahead of his scion in 1993.) Soderstrom earned rave reviews for the hitting ability he displayed in his professional debut, though he needs time behind the plate in games before anyone will anoint him as the A's catcher of the future.

Raúl Alcántara RHP
Born: 12/04/92 Age: 28 Bats: R Throws: R
Height: 6'4" Weight: 220 Origin: International Free Agent, 2009

YEAR	TEAM	LVL	AGE	W	L	SV	G	GS	IP	H	HR	BB/9	K/9	K	GB%	BABIP
2018	NAS	AAA	25	5	7	5	32	10	83[1]	100	10	1.5	5.7	53	38.0%	.319
2019	KT	NPB	26	11	11	0	27	27	172[2]	189	15	1.0	5.2	100		
2020	DOO	NPB	27	20	1	0	31	31	198[2]	174	12	1.0	8.2	182		
2021									No projection							

Comparables: Jake Faria, Keury Mella, David Paulino

The list of players booted off of a roster to make room for Odrisamer Despaigne is as long as it is undistinguished—at least, it was until the KT Wiz sent Alcantara packing. The right-hander didn't pitch *badly* in 2019, but his performance fell short of the standard expected from foreign signings, and thus Doosan's decision to sign him for 2020 came as a surprise. But Alcantara thoroughly justified the Bears' faith, finishing with 20 wins and a 2.54 ERA across 198 innings, a herculean effort that netted him the Choi Dong-won award for the league's best pitcher. The mystery here isn't that he succeeded, as good control and the best velocity in the league is a pretty reliable formula. No, the real question is what happened in 2019, when all of those attributes produced a mediocre ERA and a 5.2 K/9? We may never know, but whatever the case, it sure seems like Alcantara is a big-league player wearing a KBO jersey.

YEAR	TEAM	LVL	AGE	WHIP	ERA	DRA-	WARP	MPH	FB%	WHF	CSP
2018	NAS	AAA	25	1.37	5.29	102	0.5				
2019	KT	NPB	26	1.25	4.01						
2020	DOO	NPB	27	1.03	2.54						
2021					No projection						

Paul Blackburn   RHP

Born: 12/04/93   Age: 27   Bats: R   Throws: R
Height: 6'1"   Weight: 196   Origin: Round 1, 2012 Draft (#56 overall)

YEAR	TEAM	LVL	AGE	W	L	SV	G	GS	IP	H	HR	BB/9	K/9	K	GB%	BABIP
2018	OAK	MLB	24	2	3	0	6	6	27²	33	2	2.0	6.2	19	47.8%	.344
2019	LV	AAA	25	11	3	0	24	22	132²	133	18	2.3	6.2	92	53.7%	.293
2019	OAK	MLB	25	0	2	0	4	1	11	19	3	3.3	6.5	8	50.0%	.400
2020	OAK	MLB	26	0	1	0	1	1	2¹	5	0	7.7	7.7	2	50.0%	.500
2021 FS	OAK	MLB	27	2	3	0	57	0	50	51	6	3.9	6.8	37	50.1%	.289
2021 DC	OAK	MLB	27	2	2	0	51	0	12	12	1	3.9	6.8	9	50.1%	.289

Comparables: Zach Davies, Daniel Mengden, Joe Ross

Judging by his facial hair, Blackburn is a fan of symmetry. It must be some small comfort as he approaches his age-27 season, then, that he does so with a matching ERA from the previous season. "Small" being the operative word there.

YEAR	TEAM	LVL	AGE	WHIP	ERA	DRA-	WARP	MPH	FB%	WHF	CSP
2018	OAK	MLB	24	1.41	7.16	86	0.5	91.3	40.4%	18.8%	
2019	LV	AAA	25	1.26	4.34	66	4.4				
2019	OAK	MLB	25	2.09	10.64	114	0.0	92.4	61.2%	24.5%	
2020	OAK	MLB	26	3.00	27.00	96	0.0	91.0	50.0%	10.5%	
2021 FS	OAK	MLB	27	1.45	4.65	106	0.1	91.7	50.7%	20.1%	42.6%
2021 DC	OAK	MLB	27	1.45	4.65	106	0.0	91.7	50.7%	20.1%	42.6%

Wandisson Charles   RHP

Born: 09/07/96   Age: 24   Bats: R   Throws: R
Height: 6'4"   Weight: 263   Origin: International Free Agent, 2015

YEAR	TEAM	LVL	AGE	W	L	SV	G	GS	IP	H	HR	BB/9	K/9	K	GB%	BABIP
2018	BEL	LO-A	21	0	0	0	11	0	11	6	1	13.9	15.5	19	52.6%	.278
2019	BEL	LO-A	22	1	0	0	13	0	22¹	12	1	8.1	14.9	37	48.8%	.275
2019	STK	HI-A	22	2	0	2	18	0	25²	14	1	6.3	13.7	39	32.7%	.277
2019	MID	AA	22	1	0	0	9	0	14¹	9	1	3.1	10.7	17	31.4%	.235
2021 FS	OAK	MLB	24	2	3	0	57	0	50	40	7	10.5	13.1	72	36.3%	.304
2021 DC	OAK	MLB	24	0	0	0	6	0	6	4	0	10.5	13.1	8	36.3%	.304

Comparables: Cristian Javier, Steven Okert, Seth Elledge

Protected from the Rule 5 Draft in 2020 but not 2019, Charles must have impressed at the Athletics' alternate site, or at least given reason for the organization to expect the 100-and-a-slider righty would hew more to the 226 strikeouts in 170 1/3 minors innings than the 150 walks.

Oakland Athletics 2021

YEAR	TEAM	LVL	AGE	WHIP	ERA	DRA-	WARP	MPH	FB%	WHF	CSP
2018	BEL	LO-A	21	2.09	4.09	80	0.1				
2019	BEL	LO-A	22	1.43	3.22	76	0.3				
2019	STK	HI-A	22	1.25	3.16	68	0.4				
2019	MID	AA	22	0.98	1.88	68	0.2				
2021 FS	OAK	MLB	24	1.98	6.49	129	-0.6				
2021 DC	OAK	MLB	24	1.98	6.49	129	-0.1				

Jeff Criswell   RHP
Born: 03/10/99   Age: 22   Bats: R   Throws: R
Height: 6'4"   Weight: 225   Origin: Round 2, 2020 Draft (#58 overall)

The A's 2020 second-round pick, a college junior out of Michigan, Criswell signed with the same organization for which his father played minor-league ball in the 80s. Featuring a relatively advanced four-seam fastball-slider-changeup mix, Criswell could stick in the rotation or have a shot to be a dominant reliever, given he touched 100 in relief during the tail end of the 2019 season. Professing equanimity regarding his eventual role and having led a faux-graduation ceremony for his Michigan teammates who were denied an actual chance to walk, the makeup appears as advanced as the stuff.

Grant Holmes   RHP
Born: 03/22/96   Age: 25   Bats: L   Throws: R
Height: 6'0"   Weight: 226   Origin: Round 1, 2014 Draft (#22 overall)

YEAR	TEAM	LVL	AGE	W	L	SV	G	GS	IP	H	HR	BB/9	K/9	K	GB%	BABIP
2018	STK	HI-A	22	0	0	0	2	2	6	4	1	3.0	12.0	8	46.7%	.214
2019	MID	AA	23	6	5	0	22	16	81^2	71	9	3.0	8.4	76	50.4%	.282
2021 FS	OAK	MLB	25	2	3	0	57	0	50	46	8	4.7	8.5	47	45.3%	.280
2021 DC	OAK	MLB	25	3	3	0	41	3	32	30	5	4.7	8.5	30	45.3%	.280

Comparables: Robert Dugger, Jesse Biddle, Nabil Crismatt

Speaking of his progression through the minors, Holmes said, "It's pretty crazy how slo-mo it is." Oh, sorry, correction here—he was speaking about an Edgertronic camera. Well, confusion is understandable at the close of a seventh professional season, though he might have broken into the majors if afforded a complete slate of games.

YEAR	TEAM	LVL	AGE	WHIP	ERA	DRA-	WARP	MPH	FB%	WHF	CSP
2018	STK	HI-A	22	1.00	4.50	78	0.1				
2019	MID	AA	23	1.20	3.31	98	0.1				
2021 FS	OAK	MLB	25	1.46	4.78	110	-0.1				
2021 DC	OAK	MLB	25	1.46	4.78	110	0.0				

Cole Irvin LHP

Born: 01/31/94   Age: 27   Bats: L   Throws: L
Height: 6'4"   Weight: 217   Origin: Round 5, 2016 Draft (#137 overall)

YEAR	TEAM	LVL	AGE	W	L	SV	G	GS	IP	H	HR	BB/9	K/9	K	GB%	BABIP
2018	LHV	AAA	24	14	4	0	26	25	161^1	135	11	2.0	7.3	131	46.0%	.273
2019	LHV	AAA	25	6	1	0	17	16	93^2	113	13	1.3	6.2	65	40.6%	.328
2019	PHI	MLB	25	2	1	1	16	3	41^2	45	7	2.8	6.7	31	33.6%	.302
2020	PHI	MLB	26	0	1	0	3	0	3^2	11	1	2.5	9.8	4	35.3%	.625
2021 FS	OAK	MLB	27	9	9	0	26	26	150	156	24	2.4	7.0	117	39.1%	.289
2021 DC	OAK	MLB	27	2	2	0	31	3	25	26	4	2.4	7.0	19	39.1%	.289

Comparables: Dillon Peters, Jalen Beeks, Ryan Borucki

The 27-year-old Irvin threw a scoreless inning of relief against Atlanta, one proud, glorious frame in which no disasters happened whatsoever. There were other appearances, but it feels rude to mention them. Irvin was optioned off the roster in late August, as middle relievers who get hit hard tend to be.

YEAR	TEAM	LVL	AGE	WHIP	ERA	DRA-	WARP	MPH	FB%	WHF	CSP
2018	LHV	AAA	24	1.05	2.57	75	3.3				
2019	LHV	AAA	25	1.36	3.94	93	1.9				
2019	PHI	MLB	25	1.39	5.83	139	-0.6	93.3	50.5%	20.7%	
2020	PHI	MLB	26	3.27	17.18	96	0.0	94.2	52.4%	14.0%	
2021 FS	OAK	MLB	27	1.31	4.35	104	1.1	93.4	50.8%	19.6%	48.6%
2021 DC	OAK	MLB	27	1.31	4.35	104	0.1	93.4	50.8%	19.6%	48.6%

Daulton Jefferies RHP

Born: 08/02/95 Age: 25 Bats: L Throws: R
Height: 6'0" Weight: 182 Origin: Round 1, 2016 Draft (#37 overall)

YEAR	TEAM	LVL	AGE	W	L	SV	G	GS	IP	H	HR	BB/9	K/9	K	GB%	BABIP
2018	ASGR	ROK	22	0	0	0	1	1	2	1	0	0.0	22.5	5	0.0%	.500
2019	STK	HI-A	23	1	0	0	5	3	15	10	1	1.2	12.6	21	44.1%	.273
2019	MID	AA	23	1	2	0	21	12	64	63	7	1.0	10.1	72	41.0%	.329
2020	OAK	MLB	24	0	1	0	1	1	2	5	2	9.0	4.5	1	30.0%	.375
2021 FS	OAK	MLB	25	10	8	0	26	26	150	138	22	2.4	8.9	149	39.6%	.284
2021 DC	OAK	MLB	25	3	3	0	16	9	46.3	42	6	2.4	8.9	46	39.6%	.284

Comparables: Dean Kremer, Jharel Cotton, Jose Urquidy

You might've heard of the Darwin Awards, but what about the Daulton Awards? They're awarded annually for excellence in Daultons, and our man Jefferies is taking one home. You might not think two innings, five earned runs and a loss in one's major-league debut qualifies one for an award, but Daulton isn't a popular name. For Jefferies, who only really came back from a 2017 Tommy John surgery in 2019, it was impressive to see a mostly on-track debut, no matter how curtailed. The A's were likely more interested in the mid-90s heat from a starter, in any case. Jefferies holding onto the award next year depends on if he can keep to the rotation in a full season.

YEAR	TEAM	LVL	AGE	WHIP	ERA	DRA-	WARP	MPH	FB%	WHF	CSP
2018	ASGR	ROK	22	0.50	0.00						
2019	STK	HI-A	23	0.80	2.40	52	0.4				
2019	MID	AA	23	1.09	3.66	69	1.1				
2020	OAK	MLB	24	3.50	22.50	116	0.0	95.5	81.1%	23.1%	
2021 FS	OAK	MLB	25	1.19	3.60	89	2.4	95.5	81.1%	23.1%	52.0%
2021 DC	OAK	MLB	25	1.19	3.60	89	0.7	95.5	81.1%	23.1%	52.0%

Eric Jokisch LHP

Born: 07/29/89 Age: 31 Bats: R Throws: L
Height: 6'2" Weight: 205 Origin: Round 11, 2010 Draft (#340 overall)

YEAR	TEAM	LVL	AGE	W	L	SV	G	GS	IP	H	HR	BB/9	K/9	K	GB%	BABIP
2018	NAS	AAA	28	5	11	1	26	23	148²	165	12	2.8	7.3	121	52.1%	.328
2019	KIW	KBO	29	13	9	0	30	30	181¹	166	9	1.0	7.0	141		
2020	KIW	KBO	30	12	7	0	27	27	159²	144	6	1.0	6.5	115		
2021									No projection							

Comparables: Jerad Eickhoff, Casey Sadler, T.J. McFarland

Despite a half-decade of solid production in Triple-A, Jokisch never really got a fair look in the majors; his only big league action amounted to 14 September innings on the last Cubs team of the pre-Joe Maddon era. After yet another solid campaign in 2018 went unrewarded, the soft-tossing lefty decided his fortunes lied in the Far East and he's proved to be an excellent signing for Kiwoom. His glistening ERA (222 ERA+!) in 2020 oversells his ability, even as he's been plenty dominant. While he doesn't miss all that many bats, he spots everything in his four-pitch mix well, and he finished second in the KBO in BB% and HR%. In an era marked by the mistake hitter, teams really have to beat Jokisch three times to score a run. In contrast to his former American employers, Kiwoom seems to know what they have: Just two weeks after the season, the Heroes re-signed him for 2021 while nearly doubling his salary.

YEAR	TEAM	LVL	AGE	WHIP	ERA	DRA-	WARP	MPH	FB%	WHF	CSP
2018	NAS	AAA	28	1.42	4.06	81	2.9				
2019	KIW	KBO	29	1.13	3.13						
2020	KIW	KBO	30	1.06	2.14						
2021						No projection					

Oakland Athletics 2021

James Kaprielian   RHP
Born: 03/02/94   Age: 27   Bats: R   Throws: R
Height: 6'3"   Weight: 225   Origin: Round 1, 2015 Draft (#16 overall)

YEAR	TEAM	LVL	AGE	W	L	SV	G	GS	IP	H	HR	BB/9	K/9	K	GB%	BABIP
2019	STK	HI-A	25	2	2	0	11	10	36^1	35	6	2.0	10.7	43	32.0%	.319
2019	MID	AA	25	2	1	0	7	5	27^2	18	2	2.6	8.5	26	40.8%	.232
2019	LV	AAA	25	0	0	0	1	1	4	6	0	0.0	13.5	6	16.7%	.500
2020	OAK	MLB	26	0	0	0	2	0	3^2	4	2	4.9	9.8	4	36.4%	.222
2021 FS	OAK	MLB	27	2	2	0	57	0	50	47	8	3.4	9.1	50	37.2%	.289
2021 DC	OAK	MLB	27	2	3	0	58	0	18	17	3	3.4	9.1	18	37.2%	.289

Comparables: Joe Musgrove, Walker Lockett, Dillon Tate

Since being drafted 16th overall in 2015, Kaprielian has pitched in just 29 games. After 2020 it can at least be said two of those appearances were in the major leagues. The velocity looked to be more or less back after dipping in his return campaign from Tommy John, sowing hope the dream of a top-of-the-rotation starter isn't wholly dead—though the better money's on waiting for a season where he doesn't pitch the majority of his frames at High-A.

YEAR	TEAM	LVL	AGE	WHIP	ERA	DRA-	WARP	MPH	FB%	WHF	CSP
2019	STK	HI-A	25	1.18	4.46	92	0.2				
2019	MID	AA	25	0.94	1.63	61	0.6				
2019	LV	AAA	25	1.50	2.25	70	0.1				
2020	OAK	MLB	26	1.64	7.36	112	0.0	96.5	69.0%	37.5%	
2021 FS	OAK	MLB	27	1.33	4.37	103	0.2	96.5	69.0%	37.5%	39.2%
2021 DC	OAK	MLB	27	1.33	4.37	103	0.1	96.5	69.0%	37.5%	39.2%

Daniel Mengden RHP

Born: 02/19/93 Age: 28 Bats: R Throws: R
Height: 6'1" Weight: 215 Origin: Round 4, 2014 Draft (#106 overall)

YEAR	TEAM	LVL	AGE	W	L	SV	G	GS	IP	H	HR	BB/9	K/9	K	GB%	BABIP
2018	NAS	AAA	25	4	1	0	9	8	45^1	39	2	1.4	6.8	34	42.8%	.274
2018	OAK	MLB	25	7	6	0	22	17	115^2	103	18	2.0	5.6	72	38.9%	.241
2019	LV	AAA	26	4	3	0	13	10	64	56	8	2.8	8.6	61	52.9%	.268
2019	OAK	MLB	26	5	2	1	13	9	59^2	59	7	4.1	6.3	42	37.2%	.283
2020	OAK	MLB	27	0	1	0	4	1	12^1	14	2	5.1	7.3	10	40.0%	.316
2021 FS	*OAK*	*MLB*	*28*	*2*	*2*	*0*	*57*	*0*	*50*	*48*	*8*	*3.2*	*7.7*	*42*	*40.6%*	*.280*

Comparables: Jeff Hoffman, Erick Fedde, Jakob Junis

DRA isn't a particular fan of Mengden's work, his resultant negative career WARP a swing of several wins from other value scales. Chalk this round up as a win for DRA, then, with Oakland designating the 30-year-old for assignment in September and ultimately outrighting him to Triple-A. Instead, he'll ply his trade with the Kia Tigers in 2021.

YEAR	TEAM	LVL	AGE	WHIP	ERA	DRA-	WARP	MPH	FB%	WHF	CSP
2018	NAS	AAA	25	1.01	2.98	82	0.9				
2018	OAK	MLB	25	1.12	4.05	120	-0.2	94.2	53.0%	18.2%	
2019	LV	AAA	26	1.19	4.22	49	2.6				
2019	OAK	MLB	26	1.44	4.83	153	-1.1	93.5	52.6%	15.1%	
2020	OAK	MLB	27	1.70	3.65	120	0.0	92.2	51.5%	19.6%	
2021 FS	*OAK*	*MLB*	*28*	*1.33*	*4.36*	*103*	*0.2*	*93.6*	*52.6%*	*17.0%*	*49.2%*

Oakland Athletics 2021

A.J. Puk LHP
Born: 04/25/95 Age: 26 Bats: L Throws: L
Height: 6'7" Weight: 248 Origin: Round 1, 2016 Draft (#6 overall)

YEAR	TEAM	LVL	AGE	W	L	SV	G	GS	IP	H	HR	BB/9	K/9	K	GB%	BABIP
2019	STK	HI-A	24	0	0	0	3	3	6	5	2	6.0	13.5	9	33.3%	.300
2019	MID	AA	24	0	0	0	6	1	8^1	9	2	3.2	14.0	13	57.9%	.412
2019	LV	AAA	24	4	1	0	9	0	11	7	3	2.5	13.1	16	41.7%	.190
2019	OAK	MLB	24	2	0	0	10	0	11^1	10	1	4.0	10.3	13	44.8%	.321
2021 FS	OAK	MLB	26	10	7	0	26	26	150	125	18	3.5	10.7	178	43.8%	.289
2021 DC	OAK	MLB	26	6	5	0	39	12	70	59	8	3.5	10.7	83	43.8%	.289

Comparables: Thomas Pannone, Bryan Garcia, Gregory Soto

Stagnation isn't really a thing when it comes to prospect evaluation; opinions are constantly shifting as new data comes in. When no data is coming in? Well, it shifts anyway, though you might not know it from Puk. For four straight years coming into the 2020 season he'd been among the top trio of A's prospects, even as injuries took most of the prior two campaigns. When a shoulder injury delayed his debut in the shortened season, then aborted it entirely, it was easy to feel the industry tea leaves shift from "someone who's going to impress when we see him" to "someone we're never going to get to see impress." It's an understandable assumption given 36 2/3 innings pitched across three years, and one that won't go away until Puk has an injury-free season, maybe a couple at this point. He'll have that chance, though—roommate Jesús Luzardo's middling but healthy 2020 would be a worthy blueprint. Besides, the A's don't mind waiting for a career to start in earnest, provided the player in question is still cost-controlled when the self-discovery is complete.

YEAR	TEAM	LVL	AGE	WHIP	ERA	DRA-	WARP	MPH	FB%	WHF	CSP
2019	STK	HI-A	24	1.50	6.00	109	0.0				
2019	MID	AA	24	1.44	4.32	121	-0.1				
2019	LV	AAA	24	0.91	4.91	46	0.4				
2019	OAK	MLB	24	1.32	3.18	70	0.2	98.9	63.9%	30.9%	
2021 FS	OAK	MLB	26	1.22	3.36	82	2.9	98.9	63.9%	30.9%	51.5%
2021 DC	OAK	MLB	26	1.22	3.36	82	1.1	98.9	63.9%	30.9%	51.5%

Miguel Romero RHP

Born: 04/23/94 Age: 27 Bats: R Throws: R
Height: 6'0" Weight: 202 Origin: International Free Agent, 2017

YEAR	TEAM	LVL	AGE	W	L	SV	G	GS	IP	H	HR	BB/9	K/9	K	GB%	BABIP
2018	STK	HI-A	24	1	2	13	22	0	29^1	21	3	1.5	10.1	33	54.8%	.265
2018	MID	AA	24	1	1	1	22	0	30	35	4	3.6	9.9	33	41.6%	.378
2019	LV	AAA	25	4	1	3	45	1	72^2	65	11	4.5	10.0	81	47.8%	.286
2021 FS	OAK	MLB	27	2	2	0	57	0	50	45	7	4.2	9.2	51	44.3%	.282
2021 DC	OAK	MLB	27	1	2	0	41	0	18	16	2	4.2	9.2	18	44.3%	.282

Comparables: Zac Reininger, Wei-Chieh Huang, Chad Sobotka

In 1666, Isaac Newton presented his theory of universal gravitation to the Royal Society in London when he was just 23 years old, foreshadowing the rough age at which people would start giving up on prospects in 2021. Consistently reaching the upper-90s boundary of his velocity range in the last few years, Romero has a chance to become a useful bullpen piece even in the comparatively superannuated years of his late 20s.

YEAR	TEAM	LVL	AGE	WHIP	ERA	DRA-	WARP	MPH	FB%	WHF	CSP
2018	STK	HI-A	24	0.89	1.84	65	0.6				
2018	MID	AA	24	1.57	6.00	70	0.5				
2019	LV	AAA	25	1.39	3.96	68	2.1				
2021 FS	OAK	MLB	27	1.37	4.37	104	0.1				
2021 DC	OAK	MLB	27	1.37	4.37	104	0.0				

Athletics Prospects

The State of the System:
Why doesn't Billy Beane's shit work in the org rankings?

The Top Ten:

1   **A.J. Puk   LHP**   OFP: 60   ETA: Debuted in 2019
Born: 04/25/95   Age: 26   Bats: L   Throws: L   Height: 6'7"   Weight: 248
Origin: Round 1, 2016 Draft (#6 overall)

The Report: When healthy, Puk has some serious high-end stuff. His fastball velocity is regularly in the high-90s, and because of his height and release point, if anything it plays up from the radar gun readings. His slider is another potential plus-plus weapon, a hard-boring pitch around 90 with significant tilt. His changeup has flashed plus too, and he mixes in a show-me curveball as well. Puk has had significant command issues, and carries some bullpen risk even without accounting for health.

Development Track: Puk hasn't been healthy a whole lot lately. He missed all of 2018 and some of 2019 following Tommy John surgery, although he pitched very well in a late-season MLB bullpen stint. He was expected to be a big factor for the A's last year, but was placed on the injured list again shortly before the 2020 season began, and underwent labrum and rotator cuff debridement surgery in September. The history of pitchers with significant shoulder injuries is … not great.

Variance: Extreme. Shoulder surgery is about as big of a red flag as you can get.

J.P. Breen's Fantasy Take: Shoulder surgery and relief risk isn't a great combination, even for someone who has the kind of stuff that Puk does. The lefty is technically still a top-100 dynasty prospect because he's one of the few MLB-ready hurlers with legit SP2 upside. Plus, the fact that the A's are already penciling him into the 2021 starting rotation only bolsters his value. But, man, I don't feel great about ranking a pitcher in the Top 100 who hasn't thrown more than 40 innings since 2017 due to Tommy John and shoulder surgery.

2   **Tyler Soderstrom   C**   OFP: 55   ETA: 2023/2024
Born: 11/24/01   Age: 19   Bats: L   Throws: R   Height: 6'2"   Weight: 200
Origin: Round 1, 2020 Draft (#26 overall)

The Report: It was nearly a dead-heat finish to see which high school position player would take the mantle as the best pure hitter of the 2020 class. Depending on the team, many liked either Robert Hassell or Soderstrom as the standouts, with both displaying aesthetically pleasing strokes from the left side. It's easy to compare the two, both having mechanically ideal swings—under control with a solid approach and already showing the prospect of big power to go along with a sustainable hit tool. Where Soderstrom is different is his defensive home, or rather, we are left with the question of his defensive home. A prep catcher by trade, he projects to handle the defensive duties fine enough, but with an offensive profile that has such a promising outlook, you'd be sorely tempted to take the development behind the plate off of his to focus on getting his bat to the majors.

Development Track: Soderstrom has seen time in the field at third base, both corner outfield spots, and assuredly could get looks at first base down the road. The unknown position debate is in the glass half empty camp, because he's not the premium athlete you can stick anywhere and expect him to flourish. It reflects more where you can hide him and let the bat play.

Variance: High. Prep catchers have a bad track record, but if the bat is good enough that they don't need to stay behind the plate (Wil Myers, Neil Walker), the outlook gets sunnier. But that just keeps Soderstrom from an extreme variance profile as he's still a prep bat who hasn't been tested in the pros yet.

J.P. Breen's Fantasy Take: <whispers> I'm not allowed to like catching prospects, but I like Soderstrom. </whispers> In all seriousness, Soderstrom has been undervalued in the dynasty lists that I've seen, as they're overwhelmingly treating him as a long-term catcher. This seems like a Daulton Varsho situation. Rank the bat. Worry about the rest later. For what it's worth, I'd rather have Soderstrom than fellow first-rounder Austin Wells.

3. Robert Puason SS   OFP: 60   ETA: 2025
Born: 09/11/02   Age: 18   Bats: S   Throws: R   Height: 6'3"   Weight: 165
Origin: International Free Agent, 2019

The Report / Development Track: Jarrett covered Puason's signing background in appropriately thorough detail on last year's edition of the A's list. On some level his prospect narrative will always be tied up in being at the center of one of the biggest amateur bonus scandals in baseball history, but he deserves to be evaluated as a prospect on the merits. Unfortunately given that his first real pro season was 2020, that evaluation remains muddled. The A's were among the more aggressive teams in baseball in terms of bringing prospects—even low level ones—to their alternate site, so Puason spent his age-17 season facing older and significantly more experienced arms. The tools flashed, the frame remains uber-projectable, he's quick-twitch enough to stay up the middle. Past that, hope for a more normal year, and a more tangible evaluation in 2021.

Variance: Extreme. Like with his fellow $5 million 2019 bonus baby, Jasson Dominguez, if I could go higher than extreme I would.

J.P. Breen's Fantasy Take: Echoing what's been written above, Puason's value is mostly treading water due to the lost season. He was a top-150 guy last winter. He's still a top-150 guy. All of the same caveats remain the same, too.

4 Nick Allen   SS   OFP: 55   ETA: 2021/2022
Born: 10/08/98   Age: 22   Bats: R   Throws: R   Height: 5'8"   Weight: 166
Origin: Round 3, 2017 Draft (#81 overall)

The Report / Development Track: Allen was a standout Cal League shortstop with High-A Stockton in 2019 despite only playing 72 games because he missed a significant part of the second half with a high-ankle sprain. He made up for some lost time at the Fall League, playing in 18 games there, and spending 2020 at the alternate site. He's someone whose plus quickness and ability to hit for average sets him up to be a top-of-the-order hitter. He really doesn't have much power, but he can probably hit a fair amount of doubles and triples. He's also a plus defender in the middle of the infield, spending a third of the time playing second base in Stockton. He's extremely athletic on the field, especially as a defender and it shows with his glovework, footwork, and transfers.

Variance: Medium. He's already shown himself to be capable in the middle infield role, but needs some more reps coming back from all the missed time to solidify if he can make it to the A's bench.

J.P. Breen's Fantasy Take: In terms of fantasy, Allen gives me David Fletcher vibes. Perhaps he runs a bit more, but I mention Fletcher to emphasize how important it will be for Allen to hit for a high average to have any relevance in fantasy circles. Without it, he's José Iglesias, circa 2016-2018. He's not a top-300 dynasty prospect.

5 Jeff Criswell   RHP   OFP: 55   ETA: Late 2022/Early 2023
Born: 03/10/99   Age: 22   Bats: R   Throws: R   Height: 6'4"   Weight: 225
Origin: Round 2, 2020 Draft (#58 overall)

The Report: What looks like an up-and-down career at the University of Michigan actually has all the signs of a development arc trending in the right direction at the right time. Criswell had been used in multiple roles on the Wolverine's pitching staff—one of the best in the country during his time on campus. He wasn't able to nail down a bona fide starter's role until this past season due to a lack of control and less-than-ideal walk rate. This stems from a delivery that requires a lot of effort to generate the mid-90s velocity and movement on his fastball. However, he was throwing more strikes in the spring with both his hits and walks allowed down from previous years while still maintaining his strikeout numbers. Reports from after the draft suggest more consistency in his delivery and his full three-pitch mix ticking up.

Development Track: There will still be concerns about the starter/reliever prognosis moving forward, but at this juncture it appears many of those questions are being answered in the affirmative towards a starting role. Criswell has the body to endure the typical workload stresses. What needs to happen to maintain this projection? The slider and changeup flash as potential plus pitches, but need more consistency to go along with improved location of his sinking fastball. With the continued cleanup of the delivery being an ongoing process, giving him an opportunity to start every fifth day and work through the routine issues will be integral to becoming the more valued starter over bullpen piece.

Variance: Medium. There's still significant relief risk but the stuff is pointing in the right direction for some impact major league role assuming Criswell keeps throwing strikes.

J.P. Breen's Fantasy Take: Mark always tells me that I'm too negative, but it seems like every decent pitching prospect saw their stuff "tick up" in 2020. I'm skeptical. Criswell has role uncertainty and a history of control issues, without the upside of a frontline starter. That's comfortably outside the top-300 dynasty prospects for me.

6 — Austin Beck   OF   OFP: 55   ETA: 2022
Born: 11/21/98   Age: 22   Bats: R   Throws: R   Height: 6'1"   Weight: 200
Origin: Round 1, 2017 Draft (#6 overall)

The Report: Though Beck's 2019 season was interrupted by injury multiple times, he has been very solid defensively with a good arm for the outfield and natural athleticism. His offense was more of a question mark due to his inconsistent production at the plate. He's got good bat speed and bat control. At times, he showed some hints of a solid offensive package. Taken together, Beck has all of the tools to be a solid outfielder, but the question remains if he can just put his hitting together.

Development Track: Beck was only at instructs in 2020, but the team was happy with his play there and he worked on balancing his contact and power.

Variance: High. No one can ever go wrong with good defense, but he still needs to polish his hitting a bit.

J.P. Breen's Fantasy Take: In terms of context, Beck has a similar dynasty value to Tristen Lutz, and their offensive profiles are relatively similar. As I'm not high on Lutz, I'm not high on Beck. The modest potential is present—and he lacked exposure to high-end competition prior to being drafted—but Beck has struggled to tap into his raw power due to swing and approach issues. On the plus side, though, the defensive skills give Beck a better chance of being an everyday big leaguer than Lutz.

7 **Daulton Jefferies   RHP**   OFP: 55   ETA: Debuted in 2020
Born: 08/02/95   Age: 25   Bats: L   Throws: R   Height: 6'0"   Weight: 182
Origin: Round 1, 2016 Draft (#37 overall)

The Report / Development Track: Jefferies spent 2020 at the alternate site, save for one start in the first game of a doubleheader. Two innings of work showed that he mostly used an above-average fastball that showed some arm-side run but was very hittable and induced a lot of fly balls. His velocity seems to be there—his fastball averaged 95 while his cutter, which is his best secondary, averaged 91. That's over a very small major league sample size, of course.

He hasn't had a full, healthy season since 2015, his sophomore year at Cal. Since then, Tommy John surgery in 2017, and some rehab issues in 2018, he needed more healthy innings in 2020. And as you may have heard, that was hard to come by in 2020. 2019 saw him throw 79 innings, but he averaged only three innings an appearance, while only throwing 3 1/3 and 3 2/3 innings once each.

Jefferies still has stuff. There's enough velocity, but he needs to work on improving his command. More healthy innings is key, and getting stretched out after that, depending on if he stays as a starter or not.

Variance: High. Having a full, injury-free season would be paramount for the young righty, but if Jefferies can stay healthy and improve how he commands the ball, he could be highly valuable on the A's pitching staff.

J.P. Breen's Fantasy Take: Jefferies is the fourth-best dynasty prospect in this system. I've got questions about the ultimate effectiveness of his fastball; however, sitting outside the top-200 dynasty prospects and on the cusp of the big leagues, Jefferies is worth adding in most formats. He should throw strikes, and the cutter could be very good. If he can post a double-digit swinging-strike rate, he could be a nice source of rates without killing you in strikeouts.

8 **Brayan Buelvas   CF**   OFP: 55   ETA: 2024
Born: 06/08/02   Age: 19   Bats: R   Throws: R   Height: 5'11"   Weight: 155
Origin: International Free Agent, 2018

The Report: A low six-figure signing out of Columbia, Buelvas isn't the toolsiest or most projectable teenaged outfielder you will find, but he's a fleet-footed, advanced defender with some hit and pop potential. He is a plus runner who already has good reads and routes out on the grass, projecting as an above-average center fielder. At the plate Buelvas wrings a fair bit of loud contact out of a smaller frame and relatively short swing, but tends to work all fields at present over trying to tap into his raw power. Overall the approach is on the aggressive side, although he's worked on taming that some and developing more plate discipline.

Development Track: Buelvas was another of Oakland's young prospects that got a fair bit of run in 2020. Spending time at both the alternate site and instructs, the present skills popped more than Puason's, but he lacks the same projection in the body and the bat. After what seemed to be a strong developmental year for the outfielder, he should be ready for a full-season assignment as a 19-year-old in 2021.

Variance: High. The present glovesmanship makes me slightly more confident in a reasonable floor that earns some MLB per diems, but he's still a teenaged outfielder without a ton of physicality that hasn't seen full-season fastballs yet. So there's still significant risk in the profile.

J.P. Breen's Fantasy Take: Mark and I talked about Buelvas on TINO over the summer, arguing that he was an attractive under-the-radar dynasty add. Why? Oakland prioritized his professional development by sending him to the Alternate Site. Buelvas could be a solid contributor across the board, with a solid hit tool and a bit of speed. The questions revolve around his power production. If he can hit 15-plus homers with a .275 batting average and double-digit steals, we're looking at a potential top-250 dynasty guy. I simply remain cautious because he hasn't even reached full-season ball yet.

9 Sheldon Neuse 3B   OFP: 50   ETA: Debuted in 2019
Born: 12/10/94 Age: 26 Bats: R Throws: R Height: 6'0" Weight: 232
Origin: Round 2, 2016 Draft (#58 overall)

The Report: Neuse turned 26 this year and has been bouncing around the fringes of Nats and Athletics prospect lists ever since he was drafted. Even as a second-round college pick, there were questions around how the offensive tools would fare, and his minor league career has been uneven in that regard. He looked like a fast-moving, hit-over-power college bat, then the bat stagnated, then the power popped in Triple-A. All along he's shown passable third base defense due to his strong arm, and he has spent time at all four infield positions in the minors—he was a college shortstop at Oklahoma. At the point where we click the shutter on this snapshot in time, Neuse has the potential for an average hit/power combo you'll want to leverage against lefties whenever possible, and some defensive flexibility.

Development Track: Neuse was at Oakland's alternate site, but got passed over for third base reps after Matt Chapman went down in favor of a waiver-claimed Jake Lamb. I suppose that's a data point of some sort. He does have a fairly open path to a 2021 bench role on the A's, at least at press time.

Variance: Medium. Neuse has some platoon issues, and may end up a short-side corner bat if he can't solve major-league righties, but if the pop isn't just a desert mirage, you can always use a lefty masher with some defensive flex.

J.P. Breen's Fantasy Take: Neuse desperately needs consistent big-league reps to determine whether he can handle righties. I'm not confident. Maybe he can become the next Jesús Aguilar, but that kind of upside is not worth rostering in dynasty without the assured playing time. Neuse might just be a low-average corner masher on the short side of the platoon—useful in real baseball, not so much in fantasy.

10 Colin Peluse   RHP   OFP: 50   ETA: 2022/2023
Born: 06/11/98   Age: 23   Bats: R   Throws: R   Height: 6'3"   Weight: 230
Origin: Round 9, 2019 Draft (#284 overall)

The Report: Peluse was a known but not significant college pitching prospect whose poor junior year probably knocked him from early on Day Two to the end of Day Two once the 2019 draft rolled around. He pitched well in the Penn League post-draft, and flashed improved stuff in Instructs this past fall. The sturdy righty was sitting mid-90s with his fastball and touched as high as 98, and his slider is solid enough at present, although it will need further improvements to be a true out pitch. The delivery is uptempo and high effort and he's struggled to consistently throw strikes because of it. It also makes a long-term starter projection difficult.

Development Track: As a college arm with an above-average two-pitch combo at the top of his arsenal, Peluse should move fast if the instructs performance carries over. It's probably worth keeping him stretched out in a minor league rotation for now, just to make up for some lost game reps, but his likely role is a fastball/slider reliever.

Variance: Medium. Health and control/command permitting, Peluse has all the tools to be a useful major league arm. But that's two things that cloud the projection, and he's yet to see full-season bats.

J.P. Breen's Fantasy Take: Yes, middle relievers who can miss bats are increasingly valued in fantasy circles. No, you shouldn't bother rostering them in dynasty until they're already producing in the bigs.

The Prospects You Meet Outside The Top Ten

#11

Logan Davidson   SS   Born: 12/26/97   Age: 23   Bats: S   Throws: R   Height: 6'3"   Weight: 185   Origin: Round 1, 2019 Draft (#29 overall)

The A's first-round pick from just a year ago, file Davidson among those with an "incomplete" report card. He's a balanced switch-hitter with pop from both sides and may move off shortstop eventually to third base, but still, he's very much one to watch. His pro debut in the short season New York-Penn League was undeniably sluggish, but he finished the second half of his games very well, looking to carry that into his 2020 campaign. If a normal season had been played, something resembling his August 2019 slash line of .301/.400/.408 would have undoubtedly run him up the list with the expanded stat lines and everything next to his name rather than as an extra guy footnote.

Oakland Athletics 2021

MLB arms, but probably relievers

Wandisson Charles RHP Born: 09/07/96   Age: 24   Bats: R   Throws: R   Height: 6'4"   Weight: 263   Origin: International Free Agent, 2015

Charles was a bit of a surprise add to the A's 40-man, although relievers with mid-90s and higher heat are often in demand in the Rule 5. Despite his dominant 2019 across three levels, the profile outside of the fastball velocity is a bit rough. Grip it and rip it mechanics mean the fastball command is below average, and his slider and split only flash. This merely starts the option clock, and Charles has had some Double-A success already, so he has time to work out the kinks to become a setup arm.

James Kaprielian RHP Born: 03/02/94   Age: 27   Bats: R   Throws: R   Height: 6'3"   Weight: 225   Origin: Round 1, 2015 Draft (#16 overall)

Somehow, Kaprielian still remains on prospect lists entering his age-27 season. After seasons upon seasons of arm injuries, he popped up in the majors a couple times in relief, sitting mid-90s and leaning on his hard slider as his primary off-speed, which was also his best off-speed in 2019. Given that he's only thrown 101 innings in a five-and-a-half year pro career, I'd probably bet on a relief outcome here, but there's still mid-rotation stuff present when he can take the ball.

MLB bats, but less upside than you'd like

Luis Barrera CF Born: 11/15/95   Age: 25   Bats: L   Throws: L   Height: 6'0"   Weight: 195   Origin: International Free Agent, 2012

Barrera was well on his way to a useful slap-and-dash bench outfielder outcome when a shoulder injury cut short his 2019 season. He was at the alternate site in 2020, and should be in play for major league reps in 2021.

Prospects to dream on a little

Lazaro Armenteros LF Born: 05/22/99   Age: 22   Bats: R   Throws: R   Height: 6'0"   Weight: 182   Origin: International Free Agent, 2016

It's not ideal that almost five years on from signing out of Cuba has a relatively advanced teenaged hitter, Lazarito finds himself in the "prospects to dream on a little" subhead. The underlying traits of a plus hit/power combination are present in the swing, but the approach even in A-ball has been so poor it's undercut the offensive projection. The defensive profile is corner outfield, so we may wake up with a start in 2022 if he doesn't hit once games resume.

Top Talents 25 and Under (as of 4/1/2021):

1. Jesús Luzardo, LHP
2. A.J. Puk, LHP

3. Tyler Soderstrom, C
4. Robert Puason, SS
5. Nick Allen, SS
6. Jeff Criswell, RHP
7. Austin Beck, OF
8. Daulton Jefferies, RHP
9. Brayan Buelvas, OF
10. Colin Peluse, RHP

If you're only going to have one non-prospect in the 25U, a potential top-of-the-rotation arm is a good pull. Jesús Luzardo was our No. 9 prospect last year. He pitched in the majors in 2019 and flashed dominance with his mid-to-upper-90s fastball, changeup, and slider, all of which look like plus-or-better pitches. He's poised for a huge breakout in 2021.

Part 3: Featured Articles

Athletics All-Time Top 10 Players

by Rob Mains

POSITION PLAYERS

JIMMIE FOXX, 1B (1925–1935)
In eleven seasons for the A's, he averaged .339/.440/.640. The last time a player did that in one season was Albert Pujols in 2008. In his seven years as Philadelphia's regular first baseman, he hit at least 30 homers, drove in 120 runs, and had a .947 OPS every year. It's been nearly 90 years, and his 58 homers in 1932 is still the American League record for a right-handed batter.

MARK McGWIRE, 1B (1986–1997)
His is a complicated legacy, to be sure, but the more restrained Bash Brother led the league with 49 homers and a .618 slugging percentage as a rookie in 1987 and was an eight-time All-Star with Oakland. He holds the franchise record for homers, 363, and his 52 in 1996 ranks second only to Foxx' 58 in A's history.

EDDIE COLLINS, 2B (1906–1914, 1927–1930)
In his first stint with the A's, he was the star of the "$100,000 infield." His .338/.420/.440 averages trailed only those of Ty Cobb, Joe Jackson, and Tris Speaker among American Leaguers. He was also second in the league with 472 walks and 367 stolen bases. In his last stint, in his 40s, he could still hit, batting .325/.452/.399. He was also a superlative fielder and remains one of top second basemen of all time.

HOME RUN BAKER, 3B (1908–1914)
His two homers in the 1911 World Series helped Philadelphia win a second straight championship, earning him the "Home Run" moniker, but he led the American League in homers four straight years (granted, with only 42, fewer than

his 54 triples) as well. More impressive for the Deadball Era, he drove in 525 runs from 1910-1914. A fine fielder, there's a good argument that he was the best third baseman in AL history until Brooks Robinson.

SAL BANDO, 3B (1966–1976)

Bando played most of his career with the A's in the run-suppressing late 1960s and early 70s. So while a .255/.359/.418 line doesn't seem impressive, in those years, at the Coliseum, his offense was 27 percent above average. And he never missed game: Only 30 A's games from 1968 to 1976 didn't feature Bando, the team captain. He was an outstanding fielder as well. Hall of Fame voters have always had difficulty interpreting the careers of third basemen. Bando is in a group with Ken Boyer and Buddy Bell, talented players who are apparently sit below an unarticulated but de facto threshold for enshrinement.

BERT CAMPANERIS, SS (1964–1976)

The speedy, sure-fielding shortstop is the all-time franchise leader in games, plate appearances, and hits, and is second to Henderson in stolen bases. His .314 in-base percentage made him an imperfect fit for the leadoff spot from which he usually batted, balanced by his durability (12 straight years with at least 587 plate appearances). In the A's World Series wins in 1973 and 1974, he hit .313/.365/.458.

AL SIMMONS, OF (1924–1932, 1940–41, 1944)

The 1930s version of Vladimir Guerrero (or Guerrero was the 2000s version of him), Simmons' .356 batting average and 1,179 RBI are the best in franchise history, and his .584 slugging percentage and .983 OPS are second to only Foxx. Nicknamed "Bucketfoot Al" because he pointed his left (front) foot toward third base at the plate, he ranked in the top ten in the league for average, slugging, and RBI every year from 1925 to 1932 and had a 1.068 OPS in the A's World Series wins in 1929 and 1930. He wasn't always an easy guy to get along with but was capable of friendship with Ty Cobb.

BOB JOHNSON, OF (1933–1942)

Johnson hit .298/.395/.506 in ten Philadelphia seasons, well above the league average (37 percent adjusted for the era and Shibe Park). The A's were terrible during most of his tenure, losing 90 or more games eight straight years. He was top-ten in the league in homers ten straight years, adept at drawing walks, with seven top-ten finishes. Johnson was slow to enter professional baseball and then spent several years in the minors, so he didn't get the call until he was 27, which accounts for career counting stats below that of most players of his abilities.

REGGIE JACKSON, OF (1967–1975, 1987)

Reggie! went on to national renown in New York, but he won his only MVP with Oakland in 1973 when he led the league in runs, homers, RBI, slugging, and OPS. The A's have been around since 1901, and Reggie was an A's regular for just eight years, but he's still third in franchise history for homers and eighth in RBIs. Jackson struck out a great deal which kept his average below .300 for all but one season of his career, but note how he was doubly punished by a pitching-heavy era and a tough park: During his first stint with the A's he hit .256/.348/.490 at home, .274/.370/.515 everywhere else. Given just slightly different conditions his peak output would have been as gaudy as that of any of the all-time greats.

RICKEY HENDERSON, LF (1979–1984, 1989–1995, 1998)

Obviously, the greatest leadoff hitter of all time. His last year in Oakland he led the league with 66 stolen bases and 118 walks—at age 39. And this discussion of postseason shares, from Mike Piazza's autobiography: "Rickey was the most generous guy I ever played with, and whenever the discussion came around to what we should give one of the fringe people—whether it was a minor leaguer who came up for a few days or the parking lot attendant—Rickey would shout out, 'Full share!' We'd argue for a while and he'd say, '--- that! You can change somebody's life!'" New York writers sometimes tried to cast him as a negative character, but it is to their eternal shame that they were only half right.

PITCHERS

EDDIE PLANK, LHP (1901–1914)

Plank is the franchise recordholder for starts, strikeouts, innings, wins, losses, complete games, and shutouts. In seven incredibly hard-luck World Series games, he had a 1.32 ERA but a 2-5 record. He was the stalwart of the A's rotation from the American League's inaugural season in 1901, pitching over 210 innings in 13 straight years.

RUBE WADDELL, LHP (1902–1907)

Granted, it was the Deadball Era, but his 1.97 ERA over 1869.1 innings is easily the lowest in A's history. His 1,576 strikeouts rank second for the franchise, and he led the league in whiffs every year with the Athletics. His 349 strikeouts in 1904 have been topped just twice in AL history. At 6'1", 196, he was big for his day and a box office draw. On July 4, 1905, he got a win in relief in the first game of a doubleheader, and in the second game, he got the win as the A's beat Boston 4-2 in 20 innings. Both he and his opponent, none other than Cy Young, pitched complete games. The only negative, and it was a big one, were eccentricities—to put it lightly—that made it difficult to keep him on the mound and led Connie Mack to sell him to the Browns.

CHIEF BENDER, RHP (1903–1917)

A member of the Ojibwe Nation (hence the unfortunate nickname), Bender's two best years were with the 1910 and 1911 World Champions, when he went 40-10 with a 1.85 ERA, leading the league in winning percentage each year. He started 288 and relieved 97 games for the A's, with a Deadball Era 2.32 ERA that's second in franchise history only to Waddell's 1.97.

EDDIE ROMMEL, RHP (1920–1931)

Rommel was the first pitcher in the majors whose primary pitch was the knuckleball. From 1921 to 1926, he was a durable pitcher, primarily as a starter, throwing over 210 innings per year. He then moved to the bullpen, relieving 129 games (starting 53) over the rest of his career. He won 27 games in 1922, 21 in 1925, and his career 3.54 ERA was 21 percent better than the league average. The most bizarre win of his 171 victories was his last: On July 10, 1932, the A's made a quick-turnaround road trip to Cleveland. In order to save money, Mack brought only two pitchers. Starter Lew Krausse was knocked out after one, so Rommel went the rest of the way. He was battered over the ensuing 17 innings, giving up 29 hits and 14 runs, but he was still the last man standing as the A's won 18-17 on (among other things) Foxx's three home runs and eight RBIs.

RUBE WALBERG, LHP (1923–1933)

His teammate Grove was a bigger star, but Walberg was a stalwart for the A's, starting 266 games and relieving 146 in 11 seasons in Philadelphia. Between 1927 and 1932, he pitched 200-plus innings each year, going 101-69 with a better-than-average 4.02 ERA. Manager Connie Mack liked to use the lefty Walberg against Babe Ruth and Lou Gehrig, resulting in Ruth hitting more bombs against him (17) than any other pitcher.

LEFTY GROVE, LHP (1925–1933)

In 1930, when the American League batted .288 and scored 5.41 runs per game, Grove went 28-5 with a 2.54 ERA and a league-leading 209 strikeouts. In the six years from 1928 to 1933, he was as good as any pitcher in history: 152-41, 2.67 ERA, led the league in wins, ERA, and strikeouts four times. A fiery competitor, he was screaming in the clubhouse after a loss when his gentlemanly manager, Connie Mack, tried to calm him down. "The hell with you, Mack! To hell with you," he shouted. Mack quietly replied, "And to hell with you too, Robert." A product of Mack's relationship with International League Orioles proprietor Jack Dunn, the only shame was that Mack didn't pick him up sooner—Grove didn't make his debut until he was 25.

CATFISH HUNTER, RHP (1965–1974)

From 1967 to 1974, Hunter was first in the American League in wins; second in starts, innings, and shutouts; and fourth in strikeouts. He threw at least 234 innings each season. He was the 1974 Cy Young Award winner, leading the league with 25 wins and 2.49 ERA, only to leave the club as a free agent over the following winter due to a contract mix-up. The irony of his loss was that he had been pitched so hard over the previous seasons (something the Yankees only exacerbated) that he had just one quality season left. He was 4-0 with a 2.13 ERA in Oakland's three straight World Championships from 1972 to 1974.

VIDA BLUE, LHP (1969–1977)

When Charlie Finley, unable to compete in the era of free agency, tore down the A's, Blue was the one guy left with the club—he would have been dealt away too, but Commissioner Bowie Kuhn got in the way. He absorbed a 14-19 record in 1977 with the worst run support in the league. Before then, he threw 312 innings as a 21-year-old in his amazing 1971 season (24-8, 1.82 ERA, 8 shutouts, 301 strikeouts, Cy Young Award and MVP). His arm held up, and he went on to throw 220-plus innings eight straight years. His big year proved to be a one-off, but he was still a high-quality pitcher in more than a half-dozen other seasons.

TIM HUDSON, RHP (1999–2004)

Hudson was with the club for just six years, but his .702 winning percentage (92-39) ranks second only to Grove in franchise history. His best season was 2003, when he pitched 240 innings and had a 2.70 ERA in the heart of the Steroid Era. Until an oblique industry landed him on the injured list in June 2004, he started 171 games, the most in the league, never missing a turn, from his June 1999 callup.

BARRY ZITO, LHP (2000–2006)

A durable lefty (34-35 starts per season, six straight seasons) with the best curveball in the league, he was the 2002 Cy Young Award winner. He was the ninth player selected in the 1999 draft, and while the A's dropped four of five Division Series while he was with the club, he had a 2.43 ERA in six Division Series starts, going 4-2. He was in the top ten in the league in innings and strikeouts four times and led the league with 95 wins from 2001 to 2006.

A Taxonomy of 2020 Abnormalities

by Rob Mains

I'm going to start this with a trivia question. Trust me, it's relevant. Don't bother skipping to the end of the article to find the answer, it's not there.

Only five players have appeared in 140 or more games for 16 straight seasons. Who are they?

It's a trivia question starting off an essay, so you know how this works: Whatever you guessed, you're wrong. It's okay. As someone who purchased this book, chances are good that you're an educated baseball fan. But the circumstances behind 2020 force us to abandon, or at least seriously question, some of our favorite patterns and crutches for evaluating the game we love.

We just completed what was undoubtedly the strangest season in MLB history. No fans, geographically limited schedule, universal DH, seven-inning twin bills, runners on second in extra innings, a 16-team postseason, a club playing at a Triple-A stadium. Some of these changes will likely persist (sorry), but we've never had so many tweaks dumped on us all at once, at least not since they figured out how many balls were in a walk.

And the biggest, of course, was the 60-game season. The 19th century was dotted with teams that went bankrupt before the season ended, but the lone season with only 60 scheduled games was 1877. That year there were only six teams, the league rostered a total of 77 players (just 16 more than the 2020 Marlins), and batters called for pitches to be thrown high or low by the pitcher, who was 50 feet away. We can say the 2020 season was easily the shortest ever for recognizable baseball.

As such, it'll stand out. Few abbreviated seasons do. Just about everybody reading this knows the 1994 season ended after Seattle's Randy Johnson struck out Oakland's Ernie Young for the last out of the Mariners-A's game on August 11. The ensuing player strike wiped out the rest of the season and the postseason. Teams played only 112-117 games that year.

And many of you know that a strike in the middle of the 1981 season split the season in two, resulting in the only Division Series until 1995. Teams played only 103-111 games that year, the shortest regular season since 1885.

Those two seasons are memorable. So when we see that nobody drove in 100 runs in 1981, or that Greg Maddux was the only pitcher with 180 or more innings pitched in 1994, we think, "Of course. Strike year."

But we don't remember other short years. You might not recall that the 1994 strike spilled into the next year, chopping 18 games off the 1995 schedule. You might've read that the 1918 season, played during the last pandemic, ended after Labor Day due to the government's World War I "work or fight" order. A strike erased the first week and a half of the 1972 season, but that year's best known as the last time pitchers batted in the American League.

The point is, while we don't remember small changes to the schedule, we remember the big ones. The 1981 mid-season strike. The 1994 season- and Series-ending strike. And, of course, the pandemic-shortened 2020 season. We won't need a reminder why Marcell Ozuna's 18 homers were the fewest to lead the National League in a century. (Literally; Cy Williams led with 15 in 1920.)

Now, about that trivia question. The five players are Hank Aaron, Brooks Robinson, Pete Rose, Ichiro Suzuki, and Johnny Damon. The one nobody gets, of course, is Damon, and a lot of people miss Ichiro, whose last season of 140-plus games came garbed in the red-orange and ocean blue of Miami when he was 42. That's half of what makes it a good question. The other half is the two guys whom many think made the list but didn't. Lou Gehrig? His streak started in the Yankees' 42nd game of the 1925 season and lasted only 13 seasons after that. And everybody assumes Cal Ripken Jr. did it, having played 2,632 straight games over 17 seasons. But one of those 17 seasons was 1994, when the Orioles played only 112 games.

My point? *I just told you* everybody remembers the 1994 strike year, but everybody forgets it fell in the middle of Ripken's streak, separating the first twelve years from the last four. Just because we recall something doesn't mean it's always at the front of our minds.

Nobody is going to forget 2020, and baseball is obviously not the main reason. But there will come a time in the future when you're looking at a player's or a team's record, and there will be baffling numbers there for 2020, and you'll think, "I wonder what happened." (Not to mention the missing line for minor league players.) Just like you forgot that the 1994 strike limited Ripken to 112 games.

Try not to forget it, though. The 2020 season resulted in weird statistical results for several reasons.

There were only 60 games.
I know, duh. But that had impacts beyond counting stats like Ozuna's home run total or Yu Darvish and Shane Bieber leading the majors with eight wins. (I know, pitcher wins, but still.)

The 162-game season is the longest among major North American sports, and that duration gives us a gift. Over the course of a long season, small variations tend to even out. A player who has a ten-game hot streak will probably have a ten-game cold streak. A team that starts the year losing a bunch of close games will probably win a bunch of them. We get regression to the mean. Statistics stabilize.

Consider flipping a coin. Over the long run, we expect it to come up heads about half the time. But the fewer flips, the more variation there'll be. If you flip a coin six times, probability theory tells us you'll get at least two-third heads about 34 percent of the time. Flip it 30 times, your chance of two-thirds heads drops to five percent.

Or, relevant to this case, if you flip a coin 60 times, your chance of getting at least 36 heads—that's 60 percent—is 7.75 percent. Expand the coin-flipping to 162 times, and the chance of getting 60 percent heads drops to 0.73 percent.

In other words, the odds of an outcome that's 20 percent better (or worse) than expected is *more than ten times higher* when you flip your coin 60 times than when you do it 162 times. Call it small sample size, call lack of mean reversion, or call it luck not evening out, 162 is a lot more predictive than 60. You get much more variation over 60 games than over 162. Bieber's 1.63 ERA and 0.87 FIP aren't something we'd see over a full season, and neither is Javier Baéz's .203/.238/.360.

Some players' lines in 2020 look normal. Brian Anderson had an .811 OPS in 2019 and an .810 OPS in 2020. (He probably would have gotten that last point if he'd been given enough time.) But there are many like Bieber and Baéz, some of them from young players still establishing their talent levels. The answer to the question, "What went right or wrong for that guy in 2020?" is most likely "Nothing, it was just a 2020 thing."

Preseason training was abbreviated for hitters.

Every year, spring training drags. Players get tired of it, fans get tired of it, and you sure can tell sportswriters get tired of it. Yes, something to get everyone into shape is necessary, but does it really have to drag on for over a month? Can't we shorten it?

The 2020 season answered in the negative, at least for hitters. Warren Spahn is credited with saying that hitting is timing and pitching is upsetting timing. It appears nobody had his timing down after the abbreviated July summer camp. Through August 9—18 games into the season—MLB batters were hitting .230/.311/.395 with a .275 BABIP. That BABIP, had it held, would have been the lowest since 1968, the Year of the Pitcher. In recent years it's hovered around .300.

It didn't hold. Play returned to more normal levels the rest of the year: .249/.325/.425 with a .297 BABIP starting August 10. But batters whose play concentrated in those first two weeks wound up with ugly lines. Andrew

Benintendi went on the injured list with a season-ending rib cage strain on August 11. His final line: .103/.314/.128 in 14 games. Franchy Cordero went on the IL with a hamate bone fracture on August 9 and a .154/.185/.231 line. Even though he came back strong in a late September return, it was too late to repair his full-season numbers.

Preseason training was abbreviated for pitchers.

Every year, spring training drags. Players get tired of it, fans get tired of it … wait, I already said that. But the abbreviated preseason was tough on pitchers, too. As noted, they had the upper hand coming out of the gate. But then they lost that hand. And then their arms, too.

The 2020 season was spread over 67 days. During those 67 days, 237 pitchers hit the Injured List, compared to 135 in the first 67 days of 2019. A lot of those IL stints, though, were COVID-19-related. Still, over the first 67 days of the 2019 season, there were 72 pitchers on the IL with arm injuries. That figure jumped to 110 in 2020, a 53 percent increase.

There are a number of factors contributing to pitcher arm injuries, ranging from usage to velocity, but it appears that attenuated preseason training played a role. A lot of pitchers had super-short seasons due to arm woes. Corey Kluber, Roberto Osuna, and Shohei Ohtani combined for seven innings, none after August 8. All suffered arm injuries. We'll never know whether they'd have fared better with a longer preseason, but we can guess how they probably feel.

Everybody played.

Rosters were set to expand from 25 to 26 in 2020, so even if we'd had a normal season, we'd have likely seen 2019's record of 1,410 players on MLB rosters broken. But due to the pandemic, rosters started the year at 30 and were cut to only 28. Add multiple COVID-19 absences and the revolving door caused by poor starts by hitters and a rash of pitcher arm injuries, and 1,289 players appeared in MLB games in 2020. The comparable figure over the first 67 days of the 2019 season was 1,109. That 16 percent increase works out to an average of six more players per team in 2020 compared to a similar slice of 2019. A future look back at 2020 rosters will include a lot of unfamiliar names.

Plus became a minus.

In advanced metrics, we adjust batter and pitcher performance for park and league/era variations. A plus sign appended to the end of a measure means that it's adjusted for park and league. It's scaled to an average of 100, with higher figures above average and lower figures below average. (Similarly, a metric with a minus is also park- and league-adjusted and scaled to 100, with lower values better.) Here at BP, our advanced measure of offensive performance is DRC+. Baseball-Reference has OPS+ and FanGraphs has wRC+.

Using park and league adjustments, we can compare Dante Bichette's 1995 Steroid Era season at pre-humidor Coors Field (.340/.364/.620, 40 homers, 128 RBI, MVP runner-up) with Jim Wynn's 1968 Year of the Pitcher season at the cavernous Astrodome (.269/.376/.474, 26 homers, 67 RBI, no MVP votes). It's not close. DRC+, OPS+, and wRC+ all give the nod to Wynn, handily. This is a useful tool. As my Baseball Prospectus colleague Patrick Dubuque tweeted last fall, "Please note that when I ask how you are, I am already adjusting for era."

The 2020 season messes up plus (and minus) stats for two reasons. First, the park adjustment was based on only 30 home games instead of the usual 81. Everything noted above regarding the short season applies, literally doubly, to park effect calculations. DRC+ uses a single-season park factor. OPS+ uses a three-year average and wRC+ five years. The figure for 2020 is suspect.

Second, OPS+ and wRC+ adjust for league: American and National. (DRC+ adjusts for opponent, regardless of league.) While there were two leagues in 2020, they were an artificial construct. To reduce travel, teams played opponents geographically, not based on league. There weren't two leagues, American and National. There were three, Western, Central, and Eastern.

That makes a difference because teams in the same league played in different run-scoring environments. AL teams scored 4.58 runs per game, NL teams 4.71. That's a small difference. But teams in the East scored 0.21 more runs per game (4.95) than teams in the West (4.74), and they both scored a lot more than Central teams (4.25). Adjusting for league misses that difference, so this book will be safe in that regard, but other sources may be distorted somewhat.

Not every game was a "game."

In 2020, the rising tide of strikeouts was finally stemmed. Strikeouts per team per game fell from 8.8 in 2019 to 8.7 in 2020. That marked the first decline after 14 straight annual increases.

In 2020, the rising tide of strikeouts rose higher. Batters struck out in 23.4 percent of plate appearances compared to 23.0 percent in 2019. That marked the 15th straight annual increase.

Both are true statements.

Because of two rule changes—seven-inning doubleheaders and runners on second in extra innings—games in 2020 were unprecedented in their brevity. There were 37.0 plate appearances per game in 2020. The only years with fewer were 1904 and 1906-1909. The average game in 2020 entailed 8.61 innings pitched, the fewest since 1899.

So when you see any per-game stats for 2020, you need to increase them by 3 or 4 percent to get them on equal footing with recent years.

Oakland Athletics 2021

Or, better, just ignore them. Last year happened. There were major league games contested between major league teams. But when you're looking at those physical or electronic baseball cards, when you're weaving narratives over why this young player's inevitable rise to stardom fell apart or why that old veteran rekindled his magic, don't linger on the 2020 line. It was just too weird.

Thanks to Lucas Apostoleris for research assistance.

—Rob Mains is an author of Baseball Prospectus.

Tranches of WAR

by Russell A. Carleton

We ask "replacement level" to be a lot of things. Sometimes contradictory things. Sometimes I wonder if we know what it even means anymore. The original idea was that it represented the level of production that a team could expect to get from "freely available talent", including bench players, minor leaguers, and waiver wire pickups. It created a common benchmark to compare everyone to, and for that reason, it represented an advancement well beyond what was available at the time. In fact, it created a language and a framework for evaluating players that was not just better but *entirely* different than what came before it.

But then we started mumbling in that language. The idea behind "wins above replacement" was one part sci-fi episode and one part mathematical exercise. Imagine that a player had disappeared before the season and suddenly, in an alternate timeline, his team would have had to replace him. The distance between him and that replacement line was his value. We need to talk about that alternate timeline.

Without getting too into 2:00 am "deep conversations" with extensive navel-gazing, it's worth thinking about why one player might not be playing, while another might.

- A player might not be playing because he has a short-term injury or his manager believes that he needs a day off.
- A player might not be playing because he has a longer-term injury that requires him to be on the injured list.

There's a difference here between these two situations. In particular, the first one generally *doesn't* involve a compensatory roster move, while the second one does. It's possible, though not guaranteed, that the person who will be replacing the injured/resting player would be the same in either case. That matters. Teams generally carry a spare part for all eight position players on the diamond, although in the era of a four-player bench, those spare parts usually are the backup plan for more than one spot.

A couple of years ago, I posed a hypothetical question. Suppose that a team had two players in its system fighting for a fourth outfielder spot. One of them was a league average hitter, but would be worth 20 runs below average if allowed to play center field for a full season. One of them was a perfectly average fielder, but would be 15 runs below average as a hitter, if allowed to play an entire season. Which of the two should the team roster? It's tempting to say the second one, as overall, he is the better player. That misses the point. A league average hitter on the bench isn't just a potential replacement for an injured outfielder. He might also pinch hit for the light-hitting shortstop in a key spot. You keep the average hitter on the roster, even though he isn't a hand-in-glove fit for one specific place on the field, because being a bench player is a different job description than being a long-term fill-in for someone. If you find yourself in need of a longer-term fill-in, you can bring the other guy up from AAA.

When we're determining the value of an everyday player though, if he had disappeared before the season and a team would have had to replace his production, they likely would have done it with a player who was a long-term fill-in type because they would have had to replace a guy who played everyday. Maybe that's the same guy that they would have rostered on their bench anyway, but we don't know. It gets to the query of what we hope to accomplish with WAR. Are we looking for an accurate modeling of reality or are we looking for a common baseline to compare everyone to? Both have their uses, but they are somewhat different questions.

Let's talk about another dichotomy.

- A player might not be playing because he isn't very good and is a bench-level player.
- A player might not be playing because there is another player on the team who has a situational advantage that makes him the better choice today. The classic case of this is a handedness platoon. On another day, he might be a better choice.

When we think about player usage, I think we're still stuck in the model that there are starters and there are scrubs. We have plenty of words for bench players or reserves or backups or utility guys. We do still have the word "platoon" in our collective vocabulary, but in the age of short benches, it's hard to construct one. It's always been hard to construct them. You have to find two players who hit with different hands, have skill sets that complement each other, and probably play the same position. In the era of the short bench, one of them had probably better double as a utility player in some way. Baseball has a two-tiered language geared toward the idea of regulars and reserves. The fact that it was so easy for me to find plenty of synonyms for "a player whose primary function is to come into a game to replace a regular player if he is injured or resting" should tell you something.

I'm always one to look for "unspoken words" in baseball. What is it called when someone is both half of a platoon and the utility infielder? That guy exists sometimes, but he reveals himself in that role—usually by accident. We don't have a word for that, and whenever I find myself saying "we don't have a word for that", I look for new opportunities. What do you call it, further, when the job of being the utility infielder is decentralized across the whole infield with occasional contributions from the left fielder? It's not even a "super-utility" player. What happens when you build your entire roster around the idea that everyone will be expected to be a triple major?

⚾   ⚾   ⚾

I think someone else beat me to this one, and on a grand scale. Platoons work because we know that hitters of the opposite hand to the pitcher get better results than hitters of the same hand, usually to the tune of about 20 points of OBP. If you want to express that in runs, it usually comes out to somewhere around 10 to 12 runs of linear weights value prorated across 650 PA. But hang on a second, now let's say that we have two players who might start today, both of roughly equal merit with the bat. One has a handedness advantage, but is the worse fielder of the two. In that case, as long as his "over the course of a season" projection as a fielder at whatever position you want to slot him into is less than a 10-run drop from the guy he might replace, then he's a better option today.

We're not used to thinking of utility players as bat-first options, who would play below-average defense at three different infield positions. That guy might hook on as a 2B/3B/LF type (Howie Kendrick, come on down!) but teams usually think to themselves that they need as their utility infielder someone who "can handle" shortstop, the toughest of the infield spots to play. If someone can do that *and* hit well, he's probably already starting somewhere, so he's not available as a utility infielder. It's easier for those glove guys to find a job. In a world where the replacement for a shortstop *has to be* the designated utility infielder, that makes sense.

But as we talked about last week, we're living in a different world. The rate at which a replacement for a regular starter turns out to be *another starter* shifting over to cover has gone way up over the last five years. There was always some of it in the game, but this has been a supernova of switcheroos. Now if your second baseman is capable of playing a decent shortstop, that 2B/3B/LF guy can swap in. He's not actually playing shortstop, and maybe the defense suffers from the switch, but if he's got enough of a bat, he might outhit those extra fielding miscues. And in doing so, he is effectively your backup shortstop.

Somewhere along the lines, teams got hip to the idea of multi-positional play from their regulars. I've written before about how you can't just put a player, however athletic, into a new position and expect much at first. The data tell us that. Eventually, players can learn to be multi-positionalists, but it takes time, roughly on the order of two months, before they're OK. But there's a hidden message in there. If you give a player some reps at a new spot, he's a reasonably gifted athlete and somewhat smart and willing to learn, he could probably pick it up enough to get to "good enough," and it doesn't take forever. You just have to be purposeful about it. Maybe you get to the point where you can start to say "he's still below average but we could move him there and get another bat into the lineup, and it's a net win."

Teams have started to build those extra lessons into their player development program. It used to be seen as a mark of weakness to be relegated to "utility player" because that meant that you were a bench player (all those synonyms above come with a side of stigma). Now, it's a way of building a team. If you get a few reps in the minors (where it doesn't count) at a spot, you'll have at least played the spot at game speed before. There are limits to how far you can push that. A slow-footed "he's out in left field because we don't have the DH" guy is never going to play short, but maybe your third baseman can try second base and not look like a total moose out there.

⚾ ⚾ ⚾

Back to WAR. I'd argue that the world of starters and scrubs is slowly disintegrating, for good cause. In the event that a regular starter really does go down with an injury–ostensibly, the alternate universe scenario that WAR is attempting to model–it makes the team a little more resilient to replacing him. And the good news is that you're more likely to be able to replace him with the best of the bench bunch, rather than the third-best guy, because the best guy doesn't have to be an exact positional match for the guy who got hurt. And that's what the manager would want to do. He'd want to replace that long-term production, not with an amalgam of everyone else who played that position, but with the best guy available from his reserves.

Now this is still WAR. We still want to retain the principle that we should be measuring a player, and not his teammates. We need some sort of common baseline, and despite what I just said, we'll still need some sort of amalgam. To construct that, I give to you the idea of the tranche. The word, if you've not heard it before, refers to a piece of a whole that is somehow segmented off. It's often used in finance to talk about layers of a financial instrument.

Here, I want you to consider that there are 30 starters at each of the seven non-battery positions (catchers should have their own WAR, since only a catcher can replace a catcher). We can identify them by playing time, and we can futz around with the definition a little bit if we need to. Next, among those who aren't in that starting pool, we identify the top tranche of the 30 best bench players, which I would again identify by playing time, and then the second and third and fourth and so on. If a player were to disappear, his manager would probably want to take a guy from that top tranche of the bench to replace him. In a world where even the starters can slide around the field, that becomes more feasible.

We can take a look at that top tranche and say "How many of them showed that they are able to play (first, second, etc.)?" and therefore could have directly substituted for the starter? How many of them could have been a direct substitute for our injured player? We don't know whether one of them would be on *a specific* team, but we can say that 40 percent of the time, a manager would have been able to draw from tranche 1 in filling the role, and 35 percent from tranche 2. But on tranche 1, we can also look at how many of those players played a position that could have then shifted and covered for that spot. We'd need some eligibility criteria for all of this (probably a minimum number of games played) but it would just be a matter of multiplication. Shortstop would be harder to fill, and managers would probably be dipping a little further down in the talent pool, and so replacement level would be lower, as it is now.

Doing some quick analysis, I found that the difference in just batting linear weights (haven't even gotten into running or fielding) between tranche 1 and tranche 2 in 2019 was about 6.5 runs, prorated across 650 PA. Between tranche 1 and tranche 3, it's 10.8 runs. The ability to shift those plate appearances up the ladder has some real value.

This part is important. We can also give credit to starters for the positions that they showed an ability to play, even if they didn't play them (this is the guy fully capable of playing center, but who's in a corner because the team already has a good center fielder) because he allows a team to carry a player who hits like a left fielder to functionally be the team's backup center fielder. He facilitates that movement upward among the tranches. We can start to appreciate the difference between a left fielder who would never be able to hack it in center (and the compensatory move that his team would have to make) and the left fielder who could do it, but just didn't have to very often.

Past that, you can continue to use whatever hitting and fielding and running metrics you like to determine a player's value, but when we get down to constructing that baseline, I'd argue we need a better conceptual and mathematical framework. It's going to require some more #GoryMath than we're used to, but I'd argue it's a better conceptualization of the way that MLB actually plays the game in 2020. If...y'know...MLB plays in 2020. If WAR is going to be our flagship statistic among the *acronymati*, then we need to acknowledge that it contains some old and starting-to-be-out-of-date assumptions about the game. We may need to tinker with it. Here's my idea for how.

—Russell A. Carleton is an author of Baseball Prospectus.

Secondhand Sport

by Patrick Dubuque

Back before time stopped, I liked to go to thrift stores. Now that I'm older, I rarely ever buy anything—I don't need much in my life, now—but I still enjoy the old familiar circuit: check to see if there are baseball cards to write about, look for board or card games to play with the kids, scan for random ironic jerseys, hit the book section. It takes ten, maybe fifteen minutes. Thrift stores are the antithesis of modern online shopping, because you don't know what they have, and you don't even really know what you want. It's junk, literal junk, stuff other people thought was worthless. That's what makes it great.

In an idealized economy, thrift stores shouldn't exist. Everybody has a living wage, and every product has a durability that exactly matches its desired life; nothing should need to be given away, no one should need to be given to. But then, thrift stores shouldn't work on a customer experience level, either. You wouldn't think an ethos of "let's make everything disorganized and hard to find" would lead to customer satisfaction, but low-budget retailers like TJ Maxx and Ross thrive on this model. People like bargain hunting as much for the hunting as the bargain; it's part of the experience, spending time as if it's a wager. There's a thrill, occasionally, in inefficiency.

In sports, the modern overuse of the word "inefficiency" is a condemnation: It insinuates that there is *an* efficiency, a correct way to be found, and that all other ways are wrong ways. It's prevalent in baseball but hardly contained to it; the lifehack, the Silicon Valley disruption are other examples of productivity creep in our daily lives. Their modern success makes plenty of sense. Maximization of resources, after all, is its own puzzle, and an industry of European board games is founded upon it. It's fun to take a system and optimize it, unravel it like a sudoku puzzle. If there's only one kind of genius, after all, there's no way anyone can fail to appreciate it.

Baseball has been hacking away at these perceived inefficiencies since its inception: platoons, bullpens, farm systems were all installed to extract more out of the tools at hand. But it's been a particular badge of the sabermetric movement, from Ken Phelps and his All-Star Team to Ricardo Rincon and the darlings of *Moneyball*. It's business, but it's also an ethos: the idea that there's treasure among the trash, something we all failed to appreciate until someone brought it to light.

It's the myth that made Sidd Finch so enticing, that fuels so many "best shape" narratives and new pitch promises. We all, athletes and unathletic sportswriters, want to believe that there's genius trapped inside us, and that it's just a matter of puzzling out the combination to unlock it. That our art, our style is the next inefficiency, waiting for our own Billy Beane. It's why we root for underdogs, and why we're excited for the Mike Tauchmans and the Eurubiel Durazos, champions of skin-deep mediocrity.

Except we aren't anymore, really. The days of "Free X" have descended beyond the ring of irony and into obscurity. There are still Xs to be freed, or at least one X, duplicated endlessly: Mike Ford, Luke Voit, Max Muncy. The undervalued one-dimensional slugger demonstrated how the game hasn't quite culturally caught up to its logical extreme. But for those who don't fit the rather spacious mold, times are grimmer. As Rob Arthur revealed several months ago, there's been a marked increase in the number of sub-replacement relievers. It's the outcome of a greater number of teams forced to play out games without the talent to win them, but it's also emblematic of the modern tendency of teams to dispose of their disposable assets, burning through cost-controlled arms the way that man chopped down forests in *The Lorax*. Stuff just isn't built to outlive their original owners anymore.

It's unsurprising, given how well-mined the market for inefficiencies has been of late. The disciples of the early analytics departments, and the disciples of those, have proliferated the league, with only a few backwater holdouts. The league has grown smarter, but every team has learned the same lesson. In fact, the phenomenon creates a peculiar kind of feedback loop: As teams value a specific subset of players or skills, prospective athletes learn to increase their own marketability by conforming themselves to the demands of their prospective employers.

And that's tragic, in the way that the extinction of animals is tragic; a certain amount of biodiversity in baseball has been lost. Shortstops hit like outfielders. Pitchers don't hit at all. Only the catchers remain idiosyncratic, thanks to the defensive demands of their position; eventually they too will be required to produce like everyone else, or they'll meet the fate of their battery mates. A perfect economy requires perfect production.

I mentioned earlier that more and more, I leave thrift stores empty-handed. It is true that I am more discerning than in the past; my bookshelves are full, and there are more streaming films than I will ever be able to watch. But there are other factors at play.

Thrift stores are, in a way, the bond markets of retail. When the economy is rough and other retailers are struggling, more people look secondhand for their products. But as recently as last year, publications were noting a reversal of the trend: Companies like Goodwill and Savers were expanding despite a strong economy. Publications credited a heightened sense of environmentalism and a rejection of cutting-edge fashion as drivers behind the increase, though the more likely answer is the modern American economy hasn't showered its favors equally, particularly among the young.

But it is more than just the economy. Baseball and thrift stores share something else in common, evident in our current conversations about re-starting the sport: They live in the gray area between public service and private enterprise. Thrift stores provide affordable necessities to lower-class citizens, and collectibles and fashion for the middle-class. Because of the success of the latter, prices have gone up across the board. Especially in terms of clothing, the middle-class flight from fashion into vintage has instead carried the aftereffects of fashion, including its costs, into a territory where people just want clothes. But there's another factor in the rise of prices, in the form of the internet.

The Goodwills of the world have grown smarter, too, employing the internet to extract full value from their detritus. Ebay, similarly, has lost much of the charm it had as a new frontier around the turn of the century. Everything has a price point now; even individual taste is no match for the algorithm, because anything rare, no matter how niche its market, is a collectible to someone.

The internet has had the same effect on thrift stores that sabermetrics has had on baseball; its equivalent to OBP was the bar scanner. As detailed in Slate, the rise of second-party stores on eBay and Amazon birthed an entire industry of used-good salespeople, armed with PDAs and scanners, buying books for three dollars to sell online for five. The author, Michael Savitz, reports earning $60,000 by working nearly 80 hours a week; he makes it clear that this is not a vocation of his choosing. It's long hours, with no real creativity or individuality, skimming the cream off of a local establishment and flipping it to someone with a little more money on the other side of the country. And once the vocation exists, the obvious question arises: why wait to put the wares out on the shelves? Why allow value to exist at all?

Nothing is ruined. Thrift stores will continue to sell polo shirts and DVDs, and baseball will continue to exist and make or lose money, depending on who you believe. But as we continue to refine our knowledge, we lose something in the conquest for efficiency, a delight born out of the unknown. The problem isn't the efficiency itself; we can't blame the booksellers, or the people sweeping freeways to collect grams of platinum from damaged catalytic converters. The problem is a system that requires this sort of profit-skimming behavior in order to feed families (or, for corporations, maximize shareholder return).

Oakland Athletics 2021

In times like these, with the 2020 season on the brink and the collective bargaining agreement close behind, it can often feel like the current situation is untenable. It can't keep going like this, even if we don't know what to do about it. But as with thrift stores, there's an equally irresistible feeling that it *has* to keep going, that it would be unimaginable to not have this broken, amazing sport. Both industries exist on an invisible foundation of friction, of chaos and unpredictability, even as both see their foundations buffed down to a perfect, untouchable polish. But if COVID-19 and its financial ramifications do, as some have suggested, make it such that the baseball that returns is fundamentally different than the baseball that came before, perhaps this is the time to lean in, and change the game even more. Fix bunting. Make defense more difficult. Create viable, alternate strategies. Add some chaos back into baseball. It's fun when no one knows quite where things are.

—*Patrick Dubuque is an author of Baseball Prospectus.*

Steve Dalkowski Dreaming

by Steven Goldman

We dream of being a pitcher, of starring in the major leagues. Depending on your age and your sense of historical perspective, you might imagine yourself as Walter Johnson, throwing harder than anyone else—hitting more batters than anyone else, too, but always feeling bad about it. You could picture yourself as a Tom Seaver or a David Cone, with all the stuff in the world but still being cerebral about it, thinking about so much more than burning 'em in there. There are so many models one could choose: You could be a Lefty Gomez, Jim Bouton, or Bill Lee, skilled, but not taking the whole thing too seriously, or a Lefty Grove, Bob Gibson, or Steve Carlton, powerful but treating each start like a mission to be survived instead of a game to be enjoyed.

Very few would dream of being Steve Dalkowski, the former Baltimore Orioles prospect who died of COVID-19 last week at the age of 80. Yet, there is something just as noble in Dalkowski's negative accomplishments—and accomplishments is what they are—as there is in the precision-engineered pitching of a Greg Maddux. You have to be very good to be that bad. Dalkowski had all of the stuff of the greatest pitchers but none of the command; his story is not one of failing to conquer his limitations, but striving against one of the cruelest hands that fate or genetics or personality can deal us: A desire to achieve great things which is almost but not quite matched by the ability to meet that goal.

As with Johnson, Grove, Bob Feller, and the rest of the hard-throwing pitchers who played before the advent of modern radar guns, we have to take the word of the players and coaches who saw Dalkowski pitch as to his velocity. He was a hard-drinking, maximum-effort pitcher who, if their memories are to be believed, consistently threw over 100 miles per hour. His was the Maltese Fastball, the stuff that dreams are made of. The problem is that velocity without command and control is still a good distance from utility. Dalkowski was the most effective towel you could design for a fish, the sleekest bathing suit intended to be worn by an astronaut, but that doesn't mean he wasn't beautiful: We can appreciate a journey even if it doesn't end at the intended destination.

Whether because of sloppy mechanics he couldn't calm, an inability to understand that a consistent 98 in the strike zone would likely be more effective than a consistent 110 out of it, or all that beer, Dalkowski could never make the adjustments that pitchers like Feller and Nolan Ryan made before him, possibly because he had so far to go: Feller, who never pitched in the minors, came up at 17 and spent three years walking almost seven batters per nine innings before settling in at 3.8 beginning when he was 20. Ryan started out walking over six batters per nine but gradually improved as his long career played out; for him to go from 6.2 walks per nine with the 1966 Greenville Mets to 3.7 with the 1989 Texas Rangers represents a 40 percent reduction. An equivalent improvement by Dalkowski would still have left him walking over 11 batters per nine innings.

Dalkowski was like *The Room* of pitchers, a player so bad he became good again. Cal Ripken, Sr., who both played with and managed Dalkowski, recalled in a 1979 *Sporting News* "where are they now" piece the occasion when the pitcher crossed up his catcher and his fastball, "hit the plate umpire smack in the mask. The mask broke all to pieces and the umpire wound up in the hospital for three days with a concussion. If they ever had a radar gun in those days, I'll bet Dalkowski would have been timed at 110 miles an hour."

Signed by the Orioles out of New Britain High in Connecticut in 1957, Dalkowski was sent to Kingsport in the Appalachian League, where he pitched 62 innings. He allowed only 22 hits in 62 innings, or 3.2 per nine, a number with no equivalent in major league history (though Aroldis Chapman came close in 2014), and also struck out 121 (17.6 per nine) and walked 129 (18.7). He was also charged with 39 wild pitches. That June, one of his fastballs clipped a Dodgers prospect named Bob Beavers and carried away part of his ear. "The first pitch was over the backstop, the second pitch was called a strike, I didn't think it was," Beavers said last year. "The third pitch hit me and knocked me out, so I don't remember much after that. I couldn't get in the sun for a while, and I never did play baseball again." Former minor leaguer Ron Shelton based the *Bull Durham* pitcher Nuke LaLoosh on Dalkowski. And yet, to see him as a figure of fun, an amusing loser, is to misunderstand something unique and strange.

Dalkowski kept on posting some of the strangest lines in baseball history. Pitching for the Stockton Ports of the Class C California League in 1960, he struck out 262 and walked 262 in 170 innings. Yet, he did improve, especially after pitching for Earl Weaver at Elmira in 1962. Weaver had previously had Dalkowski at Aberdeen in 1959, but wasn't ready to grapple with him then. This time he was. "I had grown more and more concerned about players with great physical abilities who could not learn to correct certain basic deficiencies no matter how much you instructed or drilled them," he related in his autobiography, *It's What You Learn After You Know It All That Counts*. He got permission from the Orioles to give all of his players the Stanford-Binet IQ test. "Dalkowski finished in the 1 percentile in his ability to understand facts. Steve, it was said to say, had the ability to do everything but learn." [sic]

IQ tests are problematic diagnostic tools, so take Weaver's estimate of Dalkowski's mental capabilities with a grain of salt. What's important is that even if he got to the right answer by way of the wrong reason, Weaver had learned something valuable. His insight was to stop asking Dalkowski to learn new pitches and just let him get by with the two that he had. Were Dalkowski a prospect today, that would have been a no-brainer: Can't develop a third pitch? The bullpen is right over there, sir. Player development wasn't like that then, but Weaver, temporarily Dalkowski's mentor, could let him work with what he had. According to Weaver, the pitcher responded: "In the final 57 innings he pitched that season Dalkowski gave up 1 earned run, struck out 110 batters, and walked only 11." It's not true—as per the *Elmira Star-Gazette*, as of late July, Dalkowski had walked 71 in 106 innings and finished with 114 in 160 innings, which means Dalkowski's control actually faded at the end of the season rather than improved—but that doesn't mean it didn't happen in some sense, just that it didn't happen that way. Again, it's the journey, not the destination, and his ERA was 3.04 so *something* had gone right.

Also along the way: The next spring, Orioles manager Billy Hitchcock was rooting for Dalkowski to make the team as a long-man—maybe Weaver had gotten through to him. There were things out of Weaver's control, like the universe's twisted sense of humor: that March, Dalkowski's elbow went "twang."

You sometimes read that it was the Orioles' insistence on Dalkowski learning the curve that did him in, but even if they hadn't learned their lesson, the injury was probably just a coincidence: Dalkowski had thrown an incredible number of pitches over the previous few years. Still, it testifies to the dangers of trying to get what you want and risking the loss of what you had. Dalkowski tried to come back, but the 110-mph stuff was gone. A pitcher with no control and no stuff is…a civilian. What followed were years of vagabond living, arrests for drunkenness. There were Alcoholics Anonymous meetings, assistance from baseball alumni associations, but none of it took. From the 1990s until the time of his passing he dwelt in an assisted living facility, suffering from alcohol-related dementia. He'd been a heavy drinker since his teenage years. As with all those pitches per game, there was a price to be paid. You make choices on the journey and some of them are irrevocable. It's like a fairy tale: "Bite of poison apple? Don't mind if I do."

In the aforementioned *Sporting News* profile, Chuck Stevens, the head of the Association of Professional Ballplayers of America, a ballplayer charity, said, "I've got nothing against drinking. I do it myself sometimes. But, I don't condone common drunkenness. We went through lots of heartache and many dollars, but Dalkowski didn't want to help himself and we weren't going to keep him drunk." The journey is *un*like a fairy tale: No one will come along and kiss it better, not if they're busy forming judgments.

In the end, we are left with a sort of philosophical chicken/egg conundrum: Is failing to meet your goals evidence of unfulfilled potential or the lack of it? Isn't what you did by definition what you were capable of doing? Or could you have broken through to something better with the right help, the right lucky break? These are unanswerable questions, and how we try to answer them may say more about us than about the people we're judging.

No pitcher ever has it easy. *All* pitchers must work hard. *All* pitchers must refine their craft. It's almost never just about *stuff*. Dalkowski dreaming is no insult to the great pitchers who made it; from Pete Alexander to Max Scherzer, they have all earned their way up. And yet, if it is true that we can only do as much as we can do, then the journey would be more of an adventure, the ultimate triumph or defeat more noble, if like Dalkowski we lacked 100 percent of the confidence, the command, the self-possession, the commitment, the resistance to making bad decisions that so many great players possess—to be gloriously human. Or, to put it more succinctly, it would be fun to be able to throw as hard as any person ever has. Even if just for a moment, and even if nothing more came of it than that, no one could say you hadn't lived life to the fullest.

—*Steven Goldman is an author of Baseball Prospectus.*

A Reward For A Functioning Society

by Cory Frontin and Craig Goldstein

On July 5, Nationals reliever Sean Doolittle said in the middle of a press conference regarding the restart of Major League Baseball and what would later be known as summer camp, "sports are like the reward of a functioning society." This sentence was amidst a much longer, thoughtful reply about the societal and health conditions under which MLB players were being brought back. It's a very similar sentiment to one Jane McManus used on April 7, when she discussed the White House's meeting with sports commissioners. She said "sports are the effect of a functioning society—not the precursor."

Both versions of the same sentiment spoke to a laudable ideal in the context of a country that was not addressing a rampaging virus, and opting instead to bring sports back for the feeling of normalcy rather than the reality of it. "Priorities," as McManus said.

On Wednesday, the NBA's Milwaukee Bucks conducted a wildcat/political strike, refusing to come out for Game 5 of their playoff series against the Orlando Magic. The Magic refused to accept the forfeit, and shortly thereafter other playoff series were threatened by player strikes. Eventually the league moved to postpone that day's games, folding to players leveraging their united power.

The backdrop against which these actions took place was the shooting by police of Jacob Blake. Blake was shot in the back seven times by police, as he attempted to get into his vehicle. He managed to survive the assault, but is paralyzed from the waist down.

⚾ ⚾ ⚾

The step taken to walk out, first by the Milwaukee Bucks, then subsequently by other NBA, WNBA, and MLB teams, was a step toward upholding the virtue of the sentiment described by McManus and Doolittle. But that sentiment does not align with the broad history of sports in this and other countries, a history that contradicts the core of the idealistic statement.

Sports have been a significant part of American society for most of its existence, expanding in importance and influence in recent years. The idea that society was functioning in a way that was worthy of the reward of sports for most of that time is laughable. Much of America is not functioning and has not functioned for Black people, full stop. The oppressed people at the center of this political act by players, specifically Black players, in concert throughout the NBA and in fits and starts throughout Major League Baseball, have not known a society that functions for them rather than *because* of them.

Politics has been part of the sports landscape since the inception of sport, but for just about as long people have bemoaned its presence. Sports are to be an escape, it is said. An escape from what, though? A functioning society?

No, the presence of sports has never signified a cultural or political system that is on the up and up. Rather, the presence of sports *reflect and reinforce the society* that produces them.

⚾   ⚾   ⚾

The Negro Leagues were born out of societal dysfunction. The need for entirely separate leagues, composed of Black and Latino players barred from the Major Leagues because of racism? That is not a functioning society, and yet there were sports.

Even the integration of players from the Negro Leagues resulted in a transfer of power and wealth from Black-owned businesses and communities and into white ones, mirroring the dysfunction that had bled into every aspect of American society at the time. Japheth Knopp noted in the Spring 2016 Baseball Research Journal:

> *The manner in which integration in baseball—and in American businesses generally—occurred was not the only model which was possible. It was likely not even the best approach available, but rather served the needs of those in already privileged positions who were able to control not only the manner in which desegregation occurred, but the public perception of it as well in order to exploit the situation for financial gain. Indeed, the very word integration may not be the most applicable in this context because what actually transpired was not so much the fair and equitable combination of two subcultures into one equal and more homogenous group, but rather the reluctant allowance—under certain preconditions—for African Americans to be assimilated into white society.*

To understand the value of a movement, though, is not to understand how it is co-opted by ownership, but to know the people it brings together and what they demand. When Jackie Robinson—the player who demarcated the inevitability of the end of the Negro leagues—attended the March on Washington for Jobs and Freedom in 1963, he did so with his family and marched alongside the people. He stood alongside hundreds of thousands to fight for their common civil and labor rights. "The moral arc of the universe is long," many freedom fighters have echoed, "but it bends towards justice." The bend, it is less frequently said, happens when a great mass of people place the moral arc of the universe on their knee and apply force, as Jackie, his family, and thousands of others did that day.

⚾   ⚾   ⚾

Of course, taking the moral arc of the universe down from the mantle and bending it is not without risk. Perhaps the outsized influence of athletes is itself a mark of a dysfunctional society, but, nonetheless, hundreds of athletes woke up on Wednesday morning with the power to bring in millions of dollars in revenues. That very power, as we would come to find out, was matched with the equal and opposite power to *not* bring those revenues. That power, in hands ranging from the Milwaukee Bucks, to Kenny Smith in the *Inside the NBA* Studio, from the unexpected ally, Josh Hader, and his largely white teammates to the notably Black Seattle Mariners, would be exercised for a single demand: the end to state violence against Black people. Not unlike the March itself, it sat at the intersection of the civil rights of Black Americans and bold labor action. The March on Washington stood in the face of a false notion of integration—against an integration of extraction but not one of equality—and proposed something different. Just the same, the acts of solidarity of August 26, 2020 will be remembered in stark defiance of MLB's BLM-branded, but ultimately empty displays on opening weekend.

Bold defiance like this can never be without risk. By choosing to exercise this power, the Milwaukee Bucks took a risk. They risked vitriol and backlash from those they disagreed with. They risked fines or seeing their contracts voided, as a walkout like this is prohibited by their CBA. They risked forfeiting a playoff game, one that, as the No. 1 seed in the playoffs, they'd worked all year to attain. They didn't know how Orlando would respond. It wasn't clear that other teams throughout the league would follow suit in solidarity. And it wasn't known the league would accept these actions and moderately co-opt them by "postponing" games that would have featured no players.

If the league reschedules the games, some of the athletes' risk—their shared sacrifice—will be diminished, in retrospect. But they did not know any of that when they took that risk. And it is often left to athletes to take these risks when others in society won't, especially those of their same socioeconomic status and levels of influence.

It is athletes, specifically BIPOC athletes, that take them, though, because they live with the risk of being something other than white in this country every day. They are no strangers to the realities of police brutality. It seems incongruous then, to say that sports are a reward for a functioning society when we rely on athletes to lead us closer to being a functioning society. Luckily, our beloved athletes, WNBA players first and foremost among them, understand what sports truly are: a pipebender for the moral arc of the universe.

—Craig Goldstein is editor in chief of Baseball Prospectus. Cory Frontin is an author of Baseball Prospectus.

Index of Names

Alcántara, Raúl 66
Allen, Austin 58
Allen, Nick 59, 79
Andrus, Elvis 14
Armenteros, Lazaro 84
Barrera, Luis 84
Bassitt, Chris 32
Beck, Austin 59, 80
Blackburn, Paul 67
Bolt, Skye 60
Brown, Seth 60
Buelvas, Brayan 81
Canha, Mark 16
Chapman, Matt 18
Charles, Wandisson 67, 84
Criswell, Jeff 68, 79
Davidson, Logan 61, 83
Deichmann, Greg 62
Diekman, Jake 34
Fiers, Mike 36
Fowler, Dustin 62
Holmes, Grant 68
Irvin, Cole 69
Jefferies, Daulton 70, 81
Jokisch, Eric 71
Kaprielian, James 72, 84
Kemp, Tony 63
Kolarek, Adam 38
Lamb, Jake 20
Laureano, Ramón 22
Lowrie, Jed 64
Luzardo, Jesús 40
Machín, Vimael 65
Manaea, Sean 42
McFarland, T.J. 44
Mengden, Daniel 73
Montas, Frankie 46
Murphy, Sean 24
Neuse, Sheldon 82
Olson, Matt 26
Peluse, Colin 83
Petit, Yusmeiro 48
Pinder, Chad 28
Piscotty, Stephen 30
Puason, Robert 65, 78
Puk, A.J. 74, 77
Romero, Miguel 75
Smith, Burch 50
Soderstrom, Tyler 66, 77
Trivino, Lou 52
Turley, Nik 54
Wendelken, J.B. 56

For the Joy of Keeping Score

THIRTY81 Project is an ongoing graphic design project focused on the ballparks of baseball. Since being established in 2013, scorecards have been a fundemantal part of the effort. Each two-page card is uniquely ballpark-centric — there are 30 variants — and designed with both beginning and veteran scorekeepers in mind. Evolving over the years with suggestions from fans, broadcasters, and official scorers, the sheets are freely available to everyone as printable letter-size PDFs at the project webshop: www.THIRTY81Project.com

Download, Print, Score, Repeat …

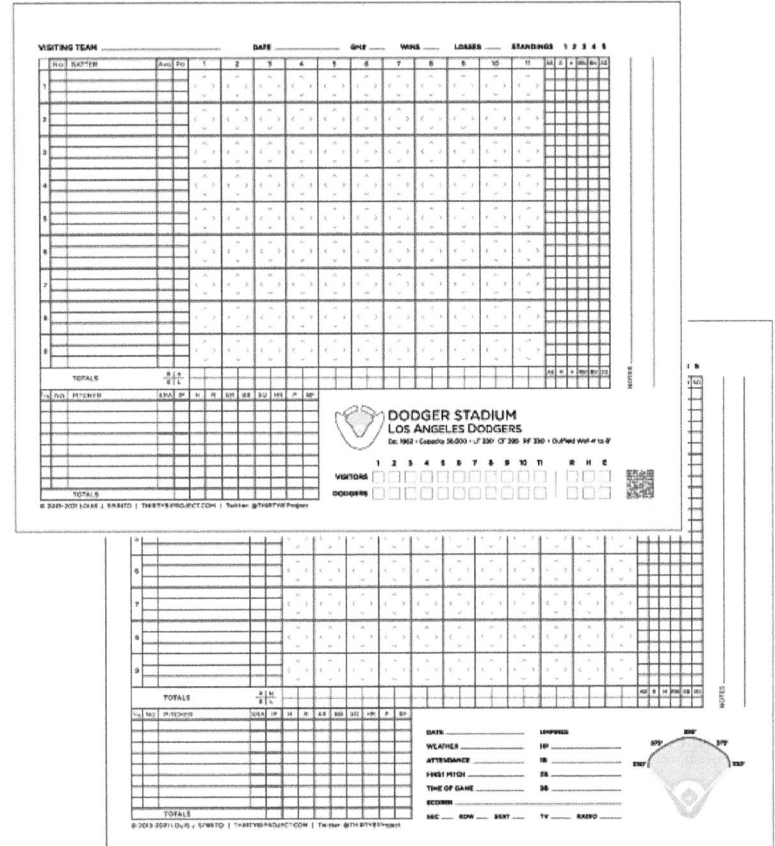

Scorecard design ©2013-2021 Louis J. Spirito | THIRTY81Project